Enter The C-Team
The Story of Thomas Taylor, Rochester Mob Associate

Blair T. Kenny

Frank A. Aloi

Narrated by
Thomas Taylor

Enter The C-Team

The Story of Thomas Taylor, Rochester Mob Associate

Blair Publishing

Copyright © by
Blair T. Kenny and Thomas Taylor
January 2020

All rights Reserved

2nd edition

ISBN: 978-0-578-63098-4

Dedication

I'd like to dedicate this book to my daughter, Laura Ann Haszlauer, her husband John, and their five beautiful children; John Jr., Jessica, Leah, Betsy, and Ben; who all wrote wonderful letters to the parole board, for my release.

And to my wife, Nancy Acker Taylor, who stuck by me throughout the years; she became my wife soon after my release.

Thomas Taylor

Table of Contents Part 1

Forward by Frank Aloi..................................page 6

Introduction...page 9

Thomas Taylor...page 10

The Hamza Shakedown..............................page 11

Prison Life...page 16

Sullivan Escapes from Attica State Prison..............page 21

Norman Huck...page 23

Italian American Club –Attica Branch..................page 29

Salvatore "Sammy G" Gingello.........................page 35

Sammy "G" Gets Cheated..............................page 40

Joey Tiraborelli..page 41

Joe and Gail Sullivan...................................page 43

Thomas Marotta..page 49

Rene Piccarreto...page 53

Sammy G's Trial..page 55

Split With Billy Barton..................................page 56

The 44 Club Incident...................................page 57

"Sammy G" Gets Blown Up............................page 59

Dominick "Sonny" Celestino..........................page 62

"Sammy G" Gets Blown Up (cont.)....................page 64

The Mahoney Connection.............................page 65

Florida..page 67

John Fiorino...page 70

Dominick Taddeo......................................page 72

The Set-ups...page 73

Enter The C-Team.....................................page 77

Table of Contents Part 2
The Aftermath

Chapter 1 The Fiorino Murder……………………………..page 83

Chapter 2 Mad Dog Sullivan…………………………………..page 93

Chapter 3 DiGuilio Turns Informant………………………page 107

Chapter 4 $500,000 Bail for Taylor…………………………...page 112

Chapter 5 More Mad Dog Sullivan…………………………page 115

Chapter 6 Thomas Pelusio ……………………………….......page 121

Chapter 7 Sullivan's Murder Trial …………………………...page 126

Chapter 8 Shootings…………………………………………...page 134

Chapter 9 Torpey and Taylor's Murder Trials …………...page 148

Chapter 10 Dominick Taddeo - Hitman ………....................page 166

Conclusion…………………………………………………page 172

Footnotes ………………………………………………..page 177

Profiles…...page 182

Appendix…….………………………………………...page 189

Forward
'Enter The C-Team'
by Frank A. Aloi
December 9, 2019

Tom Taylor and I go back decades. I represented him now and again for appeal work. I also represented him when he was incarcerated for "misunderstandings" he had with Corrections Officers that required quiet "mediation." He was more than an acquaintance before the murder conviction that landed him in jail for 25 years to life. I would run into him now and again in the bars and after hours clubs that were part of Rochester, "after dark." Maybe Curt Gerling was mostly right calling Rochester "Smug Town USA," but there was an underside and it erupted into the bone chilling violence of the 60s, 70s, and 80s. Tommy Taylor skillfully navigated his way through the minefield that was the shifting loyalties of the "alphabet wars," managed to survive more or less intact, did his time, redefined himself, and was granted a surprising "second act" after his release.

There were times when a "look" from Tom would tell me to head for the exit because bad things were likely to happen sooner, rather than later. And there were other times when his sense of humor would shine through. I recall an afternoon at the bar in Tommy Izzo's East Avenue bar/restaurant (his second bar/restaurant), the same Tommy Izzo that pulled Tom Taylor out of the vehicle the night Sammy "G" Gingello was killed by a car bomb. I walked in and Tommy Izzo was behind the bar. Tommy Taylor and Bobby Comfort sat at the very end of the bar closest to the entrance. Just around the corner of the bar sat a very attractive woman dressed to the "nines" with a large leather handbag she placed on the bar between her and Taylor and Comfort. I took the third seat at the end of the bar closest to the wall. Tommy Izzo served a round on the house and Tommy Taylor asked him to include the lady. She graciously accepted the drink. Bobby Comfort made a toast "to crime and punishment," and everyone raised their glass to take a sip. Bar conversation is usually animated, but not this day. Mostly Tom Taylor and Bobby Comfort would lean into each other and whisper; then again, they'd become loudly boisterous. Tommy finally smiled at the lady and said, "Maybe you need to take a sound check?" She laughed, actually stayed for another drink, gingerly picked up her bag, and took her leave. Tommy Taylor laughed, explaining, "She's part of the surveillance. Probably a 'Fed,' but maybe local."

I spent many afternoons visiting Tommy when he was doing time after the murder conviction. The conversation covered news of the day, families, sports, and war stories about the way it was on the streets before his conviction. His recall of faces, times, places and events, is photographic, and he's a natural story teller. Even in jail he moved some pieces on the board, to keep me out of harm's way. For reasons I still do not understand, I offended a client, Paul Comfort (Bobby's younger brother). Paulie was bound and determined to give me more than a proverbial "slap." Tom was my "rabbi," playing defense attorney for me with Paulie when they were doing time together, and even after that when they both had been released. Thanks to Tom Taylor there never was any "explosion" between Paulie Comfort and me.

Back in the day there were two Tommy Taylors. Tom Taylor was always a "good neighbor." Never through the years when Tom was page one news, with alleged involvement with murder and mayhem, did any neighbor come forth with a complaint about Tom Taylor, the guy who lived next door. On one occasion Tom's intrepid defense attorney of choice, John Speranza, had the opportunity to contest a disparity in the bail set for Tom Torpey and Tom Taylor, the "two T's" and alleged co-conspirators in a murder for hire prosecution. Torpey's bail was set at $200,000, Taylor's at $500,000 because prosecutors deemed Taylor to be a greater menace to society than Torpey. Taylor asked Speranza to have an investigator canvass his neighbors, to ask them whether they thought living close to Taylor put them at any risk. The investigation randomly contacted 12 families that resided near Taylor. Twelve affidavits were taken from neighbors, each one concluding that Tom Taylor was a "good neighbor," "always Helpful," and never "hurt anyone." That sealed the deal in court. The judge reduced Taylor's bail to $200,000, the same bail set for his alleged partner in crime, Tom Torpey.

Tom Taylor was fiercely protective of family, and did everything he could to insulate them from the inevitable consequences of his scrapes with the law. On the streets, Tom Taylor backed up to no man. Without doubt many of his choices were bad ones, and Tom would be the first one to tell you that. He was a gangster, plain and simple. People were badly hurt, people died. He pulls no punches in his book. His recollections of his crimes and punishment make for riveting reading. But consider how thin the course of one's life truly is. Tom Taylor wanted to join the Marines when he was 16, and his father pulled him out before he crossed the line and took the oath. What would his life had been like had the U.S. Marine Corp shaped him rather than the mean streets of Rochester back in the day?

After his release from prison, Tom Taylor stayed clean. Tom is happily married to the girl who waited for him. His children and grandchildren adore him. The "good man" that he always was, but never could admit to, is now center stage in his "second act."

*Frank A. Aloi is a local Attorney at Law, living in Rochester, N.Y. He has represented numerous organized crime figures during his lengthy career, including Thomas Taylor. Frank is also the author of "The Hammer Conspiracies," the first book ever written about the Rochester Mafia, in 1982.

Introduction

Enter The C-Team, the Story of Thomas Taylor, Rochester Mafia Associate is written in two parts. Part 1 is the story of Thomas Taylor, told in the first person as Tom recalls events from his memory. Tommy Taylor describes his close friendship to Sammy Gingello and recalls his memories of the tragic night Sammy died by car bomb. Taylor recalls the horror of sitting in the passenger seat, right next to Sammy, that fatal evening.

Part 2, titled the "aftermath," is the documentation of the fallout created from Taylor's last act of his criminal career, which was the murder of John Fiorino, Rochester Mafia Captain. The second part of the book includes not only all the trials associated with Fiorino's murder, but also the retribution that followed.

The second part of "Enter The C-Team" is presented in a similar fashion as "The Rochester Mob Wars" and "The Black Hand Society of Rochester," the author's previous works. The chronological collection of newspaper articles both confirms Thomas Taylor's version of events, and places a timeline on each of those events.

Thomas Taylor

Tommy Taylor began his long, extensive criminal career in the early 1960s, serving eight years in Attica State Prison for an extortion attempt on a local Rochester, N.Y. Numbers Banker named Abe Hamza. Unbeknownst to Taylor, Hamza was protected by both the local police, namely Rochester Vice-Squad Detective Lucian DiGiovanni, and the Rochester Mafia.

Prior to Taylors incarceration he worked in construction and became close friends with Salvatore "Sammy G" Gingello, the then future Rochester Mafia Boss. Following Taylors's release from prison he learned that "Sammy G" was now "The Man" in Rochester. When Sammy went to prison for the Massaro murder, Taylor became an active A-Team member, fighting with them (A-Team) for 14 months until Gingello's release.

Shortly thereafter, Tommy Taylor became employed as Sammy G's bodyguard and driver. Serving in that capacity, Taylor narrowly escaped death on the tragic night of April 23, 1978, when Sammy was murdered by a car bomb. Taylor was sitting in the passenger seat at the time of the explosion, at Sammy's request. Normally, Taylor would have been driving.

After Sammy's death, Taylor fell out of favor with several members of the Rochester Mafia and no longer had the protection of "Sammy G." The friction became so intense that more than one attempt was made on his life. At one point Taylor had a "contract" put out on his life and on another occasion he was almost "taken for a ride," but feigned illness in order to escape.

Taylor's friend, Thomas Torpey, was refusing to pay his "vig" and was being threatened by John Fiorino, Rochester Mafia Captain. His other friend, Norman Huck, had already been murdered by the Mob.

Enter the C-Team...Here is his story...

The Hamza Shakedown

Everybody hears the beat of their own drum. I followed mine into Attica State Prison in 1965 along with two others, Al Mancuso and Benny Morganti, for shaking down a numbers Banker.

We figured we would have to contend with the local Mob if there were any beefs. As it turned out, there was a beef, but it wasn't with the Mob per se. Much to our surprise, the numbers Banker was protected by the local cops.

Jake Russo, Boss of the Rochester Mafia in the early 1960s.

They dressed the shakedown up with legal terms like attempted extortion and attempted grand-larceny. By trick and device, the winning ticket being the device, instead of bullets, the cops being the Mob's bullets.

Jake Russo was the supposed "Boss" at the time. Jake couldn't face us on his best day, so in comes the vice-squad, Detective-Sargent Lucien DiGiovanni with his crew. DiGiovanni was there to kill us, not to arrest us!

He could easily have gotten away with it too. Al Mancuso had just been acquitted of robbery/murder charges 14 days earlier. Despite the jury's malfeasance, Mancuso was considered by the police to be psychotic, armed, and dangerous.

Mancuso allegedly murdered a man during the course of an armed robbery. He was defended by attorney Tom Presutti, and acquitted of first-degree murder for the robbery and murder of Ben Oken, the owner of Oken Paper Company located on Oak Street.

The Banker

The "Numbers Bank" (person who financed the numbers racket) originally was a man named "Big Babe" Blandino. When Big Babe passed away, Abe Hamza took it over from Lil Babe Blandino.

Benny Morganti allegedly cleared it (the shakedown) with Jake Russo. Russo informed Benny that Abe Hamza was not under his protection. So Benny lined up one of Hamzas runners, a man named Andrew Jackson, to take the bet and write the ticket.

Abe Hamza, the Numbers Banker

Jackson wrote a winning numbers ticket, after the fact. The extraordinarily large bet would have earned the ticket holder $10,000, that was the shakedown. But in the end, Jackson wound up turning "States Evidence," and testified against us.

So there we were in the driveway of Abe Hamza the Banker, with his numbers runner, demanding to get paid on our ticket. All of a sudden we were surrounded by cops on foot with shotguns, six total, who surrounded our car, ordering us to get out.

Lucien DiGiovanni Vice-Squad Detective

Once we were out of the car, the cops then ordered us to get on our knees. Defiantly, Al Mancuso spits and says very loudly, "I get on my knees for no man."

At that point, Detective Sergeant Lucien DiGiovanni and his partner exchanged looks. I read the looks to mean "are you ready?" I suddenly got a cold feeling in the pit of my stomach. We were certain that they (the cops) intended to execute us on the spot.

As I was being taken out of the car I

happened to look up and I saw two men across the street who were watching the entire event unfold before their eyes from a second story window. So I began yelling, "Hey, we haven't done anything. Ask those two guys across the street looking out that window over there." I was pointing to the two potential witnesses across the street.

The cops looked up at the window and saw the witnesses and then again exchanged glances with each other for the second time. I read the second glance to mean that whatever was originally planned was now called off due to the witnesses, who turned out to be a father and son getting ready for work at about 5:30 or 6 a.m.

I shudder to think about what would have happened if the two men were not looking out their window precisely at that exact time. Considering Al Mancuso's reputation for being psychotic, armed and dangerous, they (the cops) could easily have killed us by claiming we were resisting, and they would've gotten away with it too!

Lucian DiGiovanni was a Detective Supervisor with the Vice-Control Unit of the Rochester Police Department.

Was there any proof that DiGiovanni was also working with the Mob and protecting book makers and numbers bankers?

Al Mancuso, Thomas Taylor and Benny Morganti in custody following their arrest for extortion of Abe Hamza, a Rochester Numbers Banker.

Buffalo Mafia Boss Stephano Magaddino and his bodyguard, Sam Rangatore, Buffalo Mob Soldier.

Yes, there certainly was. About a year after the Hamza incident, the FBI showed up in Rochester. They were following Sam Rangatore, a Mafia Soldier from Stephano Magaddino's Niagara Falls crew who had traveled to Rochester. Rangatore was in town to keep an eye on a secret meeting between Detective Lucian DiGiovanni and Frank Valenti, Rochester's new Mafia Boss.

While the FBI was surveilling Rangatore they inadvertently stumbled upon the DiGiovanni/Valenti meeting, which took place in the back room of a joint on State Street. The meeting was not sanctioned by the police department nor were any of DiGiovanni's supervisors informed of the meeting.

We knew that any potential problems we would have with this caper would come from the Mob. Since contriving a numbers lottery was a crime we did not expect them (the Hamza's) to call the law. But that is exactly what they did because "the law" (DiGiovanni) was with the Mob, and provided their (the Hamza's) protection.

Lucien DiGiovanni (left), head of the Vice Control Unit and his partner, John Lipari (right), hand in their resignations following claims of misconduct after the pair were caught secretly meeting with Frank Valenti, Boss of the Rochester Mafia, on June 19, 1965.

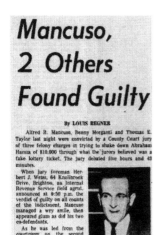

Mancuso, 2 Others Found Guilty

By LOUIS REGNER

Alfred R. Mancuso, Benny Morganti and Thomas E. Taylor last night were convicted by a County Court jury of three felony charges in trying to shake down Abraham Hamza of $10,000 through what the jurors believed was a fake lottery ticket. The jury debated five hours and 43 minutes.

When jury foreman Herbert J. Weiss, 64 Knollbrook Drive, Brighton, an Internal Revenue Service field agent, announced at 9:50 p.m. the verdict of guilty on all counts of the indictment, Mancuso managed a wry smile, then appeared glum as did his two co-defendants.

As he was led from the courtroom on the second floor of the Hall of Justice

July 9, 1964 D&C

So, instead of getting shot with bullets, we were "shot" with indictments. Following a short trial we were all slapped with outrageous sentences. Al Mancuso received 20-26 years; Benny Morganti, 15-16 years, and I was sentenced to seven and 1/2 to 12 years in Attica State Prison.

The prosecution had offered me a deal. They would allow me to plead guilty to a misdemeanor charge. But the deal had been offered to me only and not to my co-defendants. I said I wouldn't take the offer unless all three of us got it.

"No dice," they said. So I refused their offer.

My father had his own heating business, "Empire State and Residential Heating." The day after we were arrested he was on a service call on St. Paul Boulevard, and the home-owner, an elderly man, says to my father, **"Elmer, is that Taylor in the newspaper any relation to you?"**

"Yes," Elmer replied, "That's my son."

"Well don't worry," said the elderly man. "That Judge Rosenthal, I put him through law school."

Sure enough, my attorney, Joe Cerruli, came to me with an offer of a misdemeanor with no strings attached, but nothing for Mancuso or Morganti. So I said, "Unless we all get it, (the deal) I don't want it."

In retrospect I often wondered if they would have done the same for me. I would like to think so!

Prison Life

by Thomas Taylor

"Days of prison, color of grey, nights full of silence while you lay. Gone is the taste of sweetness of life, in its place, foulness and strife!

"Marching in lines with numbers for names, faces in blue, glowing in your shame! For what purpose is all this for? But to wet the appetite of a whore?

"Justice is the name she seduces by, while she plays her sickness, with unseeing eyes. For all your days prepare, and treat them each alike.

"When you are, the anvil bear, and when you are the hammer strike!"

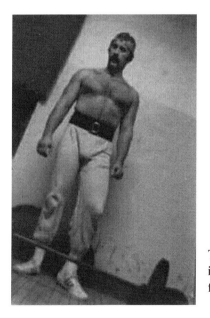

So, how does one survive in prison when every day you are completely surrounded by psychos? You "crew up." You watch each other's back. Besides spending my time with appeals, I played football and lifted weights.

Thomas Taylor lifting weights in Attica Prison with a broken foot in 1966.

I "crewed up" with a guy out of Brooklyn, N.Y. named Joe Sullivan. Myself and a few others put together a prison football team. Our team represented A-Block and was named "The Centurions," (Captain of 100). We played full contact football.

For five straight years "The Centurions" went undefeated with zero ties. Joe Sullivan did not join our team until the fourth season. He tried out for half-back and became the starter. He was fast on his feet and could turn and spin on a dime. But best of all,

Attica State Prison team photo of "The Centurions." We were the champions for 1964, 1965, and 1966. Thomas Taylor is #29 and Joe Trieste is in the top row third from the left with only his head showing.

he could take hard hits and keep on playing. I was a pulling offensive guard. Once I was able to get Sully through the hole and past the line-backer, more often than not, he would score.

Joe was doing time for manslaughter, after standing trial for murder. He shot a guy in a bar who was the father of eight children. (I found this out later.) He then held the bar up and fled to New Jersey where he started robbing Western Unions before getting arrested.

After doing his time there in New Jersey for the robberies he was sent to New York to face the homicide charges. During the murder trial, the prosecutor and Joe began arguing about President Kennedy somehow. Later, the prosecutor allegedly purposely said something negative about Kennedy to irk Sullivan while he was on the witness stand, in order to elicit a violent response.

Joe smashed his fist on the lectern in anger. But the prosecutor's ploy had the complete opposite effect of what was intended. The jurors returned with a manslaughter verdict instead of a murder verdict. Apparently the prosecution had overlooked some Kennedy sympathizers empaneled on the jury.

So, when we weren't in our assigned programs we'd be outside for recreation. If we weren't lifting weights or playing sports we'd be sitting around our spot with the rest of the crew, "Bullshitting."

When I was on the street I used to pick my friends and my crime partners by how they treated their family members, wives, mothers, siblings, etc. If they didn't treat them right you didn't have a chance because you were only a friend!

I should have followed my own advice that one day when Sullivan asked me if I loved my mother! Man, if that wasn't a weird question. "Of course," I said, "Why do you ask?'

"I hated mine," he says.

I should have cut ties right then and there and followed my regular way of selecting friends. But curiosity got the best of me and I asked him why?

So, Sully tells me about his father who was a cop but was now dead. His mother had a framed picture of him in uniform and every time he (Sully) did something wrong or she thought he did something wrong she would make him kneel in front of his father's picture. Then she would slap him in the back of the head while berating him that he'd never be half the man his father was!

So, of course Sullivan hated his mother. But what was worse he hated cops, women in general, and even children too. Otherwise how could he possibly do the things he did after he was eventually released from prison the first time.

But while we were there, our main topic of conversation was escape. We were always looking for different ways to get out of there, besides appeals. When I was working in the butcher shop, which was located in the storehouse, I had found a way out, or so I thought.

I made my move on a Sunday morning. I was a B-Block Porter at the time. There were three of us and we drew our mops out of a garage area where they worked on engines. In that area there was a seven foot wooden cabinet where tools were kept.

When we were done working that day I held back while the other two guys went back to the block. I broke into the cabinet for a crowbar, a two pound sledgehammer, and a steel chisel that I needed to further my plan.

The garage was directly next to the storehouse, which was always empty on Sunday. I pried open a door there because upstairs there were ropes, ladders, and other tools. My plan was to obtain the ropes, and tie the crowbars together with the ropes forming a makeshift grappling hook. The chisel and hammer I needed to break a chain that was locked around a fence with access to the unmanned tower that I needed to scale for freedom.

But alas, "the best laid plans of mice and men." The very

last door that I needed to get through in the storehouse was a large steel door in a big steel frame! How did I ever overlook that?

It was back to square one. But I had to get out of that area and back to my block, immediately before they missed me, and I did. But come Monday morning it was obvious that things had been broken into, the tool cabinet, the storehouse, etc.

Out of the three inmates that had access to that area and were back there that particular Sunday morning, they figured I was the most likely suspect. So they searched my cell and then used a small piece of flint with a hole in it that was used for a hot-plate to send me to the box.

The Attica prison riots occurred on Sept. 9, 1971, exactly five months after Joseph Sullivan escaped. The picture above was taken four days later, on Sept. 13, 1971, when State Police retook the prison.

(Mad Dog) Sullivan Escapes From Attica State Prison

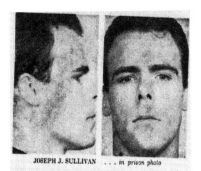

Attica Escapee Sought Here

Joseph Sullivan was the first and only man to escape from Attica State Prison, on April 9, 1971, by hiding under sacks of flour on a delivery truck.

I related that episode to Joe Sullivan a few years later and he used that to cover the real way he got out, when on **April 9, 1971,** he became the first and only man to ever escape from Attica State Prison, a maximum security prison. He was working in the storehouse at the time of his escape, along with a good friend of ours from Rochester, N.Y., Liam McGee, an Irish folk singer from Ireland.

All trucks coming to the storehouse were unloaded. So when a truck came in the guard would station himself so he could watch the dock and workers unloading the truck. On this particular day the guard was being entertained by Liam playing his guitar as the truck was being unloaded of flour sacks.

While that was going on, Sullivan was able to get the other guys to cover him with bags of flour, just before they were done unloading, and unbeknown to the guard who was busy watching Liam play. Once the truck was done, the guard called the back gate to inform them that he had checked the back of the truck and it was alright to let it out of the gate to the outside.

Once Sullivan was able to get out of the truck he made a phone call to the sister of two brothers from Utica to come get him. He stayed with her for awhile before going to New York to get busted. The brothers were doing time with us. They had killed a guy that raped their sister. Brothers Darryl and Gary Kruse.

Joe Sullivan, Escapee from Attica, is Captured

May 18, 1971, Joseph Sullivan is led through door of Bureau of Special Services State Parole Board, at 314 West 40th St., by Dir. of the Bureau, John McCarthy.

Several days after his escape, there were reports of sightings of Joe Sullivan in Rochester, N.Y. where his sister was believed to be living. Then three weeks later the search was narrowed to New York City after a citizen recognized him from a photograph in lower Manhattan.

Approximately five weeks after his escape, officers executed a search warrant on a Greenwich Village apartment, on **May 18, 1971**, capturing Sullivan. When he was caught, Sullivan was carrying a sawed-off shotgun and a box of ammunition in a suitcase. (47)

Joe was unaware that while he was on the run an appeal had been granted for his manslaughter conviction, but he was "unavailable" for court and the appeal was dismissed. After his capture, Sullivan's attorney refiled the appeal, based on its own merits.

Norman Huck

Norman Huck

When we were talking in the yard once I had mentioned one of my friends on the street getting whacked in the head, (Huck). Sullivan just looked at me and asked, "Is that the end of it?"

"No Joe," I answered.

The friend I was talking about with Joe, the friend who was whacked, was Norman Huck. They had shot him in the back of the head. Norm was a big tough man, who could punch like a mule. He was an orphan being raised in St. Joseph's Villa, an orphanage in Rochester, N.Y.

He was a loyal friend and that's what got him killed. We were in the Italian Village on Main Street one night having a few pops. There were three guys sitting at a corner table who watched us as we entered.

We didn't know them so we kept walking towards the bar and ordered a drink from the bartender. While doing so the waitress approached us, asking if we would like a drink on Jake Russo.

"Who," asked Norm?

"Jake Russo," the waitress responded as she pointed Jake out. Norm Huck then says, "Yes, give us a bottle of your best champagne."

The waitress gets a look on her face that says this isn't going to be good as she goes over to Jake's table to relay the message. Russo tells her its okay as he looks over at us and smiles with a wave. I waved back and turned to Huck, asking, "What's up?"

"Watch my back Tommy, I'll explain later," he says.

The waitress came over with the champagne, container stand and glasses.

"Shall I pour?" she says.

"I'll pour," says Huck as he picks up the bottle and walks over to Jake Russo's table.

Russo had a big smile on his face. He was sitting in between two other guys and I know he must of thought that Huck came over to thank him. Instead of thanking him, as Norm reached him he turned the bottle upside down, pouring it over his (Jake's) head and shoulders, while saying in a loud voice,

Charles "Chip The Wolf" LaPlaca

"I wouldn't have a drink bought by you, you S.O.B., I am a good friend of "Chip the Wolf."

As Huck was doing this I ran over by the two guys with Russo in case they got any ideas about putting their hands on Huck. But, they did not want any part of it.

"Chip the Wolf's" real name was Charles LaPlaca. He was doing life in Auburn Prison where Norm was. Jake Russo was involved in LaPlaca's crimes somehow, one of which was murder. He (LaPlaca) stuffed the decedent in a snow bank. He was sentenced to life.

A card let alone a money order or package, that was Charlie LaPlaca's complaint. He felt that he was not adequately taken care of after he went to prison and the person who was supposed to be taking care of him, was Jake Russo.

While in prison, Chip had taken Norm Huck under his wing and they became fast friends. Although there was quite an age difference, they were both from Rochester and Norm was a "Stand up guy!" so Chip poured all his anger out on Huck about Jake Russo. (48)

> **Charles "Chip The Wolf" LaPlaca** was born in approximately 1905. His brother Frank belonged to a Black Hand gang. "Chip The Wolf" was well known for his own lengthy police record. He had been arrested 11 times, twice serving time in state prison, before his 65 year to life sentence for murder in 1943. He served 30 more years before being paroled in 1972. He was discharged from parole in 1977 to Brooklyn, N.Y. where Sal Lombardo, Capo in the Gambino Crime Family, set him up with a house and a girlfriend.

Dominick "The Deacon" Allocco

Some time after the Huck and Russo incident at the Italian Village we were at a watering hole on State Street called El Popagallos, which was run by Bob Fafone. We were having a drink at the bar and up comes this big heavy set guy (Dom Allocco). He walks over to Huck and says that he's the "Deacon" and the boys would like to have a talk with him. He tells Huck that he will take him over to them.

"By boys," says Norm, "Do you mean Jake Russo?"

The Deacon nods his head.

Norm says, "I am not going to be able to make it but could you give him this from me?" As he is saying that he hits Allocco with a right hook that sends him head over heals into the corner and out for the count!

That was Norm. he got two and 1/2 to five years for the Keyboard Lounge shakedown and Mancuso, Morganti, and I were sentenced for the Hamza fiasco. Norm was released before we were. I sent him a message not to trust anyone.

But, Norm's downfall was that he had no fear. Jake Russo could not control the town (Rochester). When Frank Valenti returned he made short work of Russo. Some of the guys that Valenti put around him were with us on different scores.

**Frank Valenti
Rochester Mafia
"Boss"
from 1964-1972**

One of those guys happened to be Jimmy "The Hammer" Massaro. Massaro, Huck, and another guy went on a home invasion score of a bookmaker named "Potato Sacks" in East Rochester. The bookmaker was not seriously hurt and no one got busted.

Now Valenti comes to town and he's organizing book makers to pay the "vig" to operate. So Massaro tells Valenti that he can rein in the East Rochester book maker. He tells Frank the story of the shakedown. So Valenti sends Chirico over to see the bookmaker. Chirico tells him, "We know what happened to you and we know who was involved."

Chirico tells the book maker that we, meaning the Mafia, can protect you and make sure nothing like that ever happens to you again. He also tells the guy that they will kill all persons who were involved (Huck) to convince the bookmaker they outlive what happened to him.

The book maker did not want any one killed, but it did not matter what the bookmaker wanted. They had to put someone in the street to show the others that you fall in line or else; and you can't disrespect them like Norm did to Russo when we were in the Italian Village.

Huck trusted Massaro as he had gone on scores with us. But in that line of work it is always your best friend that offs you. One night Massaro and Chirico went looking for Norm and found him over at the "Fountain Blue" on Ridge Road. Chirico was good with a deck of cards. So one of Norm's moves was to go with a card mechanic when he was going to "bust a game out" just to make sure that if anyone caught the moves, they could get out of the place without getting roughed up, but still make it out with the money!

Dominic Chirico Rochester Mafia "Captain"

Vincent "Jimmy The Hammer" Massaro

So Massaro tells Huck that we got a game and they need him to come along in case anything goes wrong. The next time anyone saw Huck was when his body was found in a ditch, with three holes in his head.

How do I know this and other mob related things? How did I get so close to the Mob? Part of it was due to my very close friendship with Sammy Gingello.

> Vincent "Jimmy The Hammer" Massaro was a "Soldier" in the Rochester mafia. He also performed the function of "Hit-man" before he himself was brutally murdered in 1973 by his fellow Mafia members. The stated reason for his murder was his constant complaints about not getting paid for arsons that he committed for the Mob and his disclosure of Mafia business to non Mafia members.
>
> Dominic Chirico was also coincidently murdered by his own Mafia members in 1972 during a power struggle for control of the organization. The new faction had wanted to murder Frank Valenti, the "Boss," but killed Chirico his bodyguard, instead.

Norm Huck was paroled from Attica Prison on Dec. 1, 1967; less than three weeks later, he was found dead with three bullets in his head, fired from point blank range.

Norman Huck, a 33 year old ex-convict, who was known as a "tough guy" and cop hater, was murdered on Dec. 20, 1967. The killer put a heavy caliber revolver against his head and fired three shots. Police called it a gangland slaying but could only speculate as to the motive.

Huck's body was found at 9:45 p.m. on Dec. 20, 1967, in an isolated area on Ballantyne Road in Chili, N.Y., but police believed that Huck was shot elsewhere and his body dumped there sometime after the murder.

Dec. 22, 1967
Democrat & Chronicle

He was last seen with Robert Comfort of Fairport at 3:30 p.m. earlier that day in Comfort's car. Although Comfort was questioned, he claimed to have dropped Huck off at a pool hall at 5 p.m.

Detective Lt. Cerretto called the murder "one of vengeance," but added because of Huck's background, there could have been many motives.

Italian American Club - Attica Branch

When I was in Attica the Italian American Organization was being controlled by the N.Y.C. inmates, and they weren't doing the right thing by all the members. So I threw my hat into the ring. Since Attica is in Western New York, I figured the organization should be controlled by Rochester and Buffalo. I became the new President, and as a consolation I appointed Jimmy Burke, mastermind of the Lufthansa Heist (portrayed in the movie Goodfellas), to the vice presidency.

There were five blocks in Attica and each cell block had a representative. With my position I was allowed to go anyplace within the facility. We had two festivals yearly with members family and friends, plus pizza and sub sales. Our staff advisor was a C.O., Matt Lapina, whose grandfather owned the Anchor Bar years ago, and was credited with "Buffalo Style Chicken Wings."

Jimmy Burke (center) in handcuffs. Burke was the mastermind of the Lufthansa Heist, which was portrayed in the movie Goodfellas. He was played by actor Robert DeNiro.

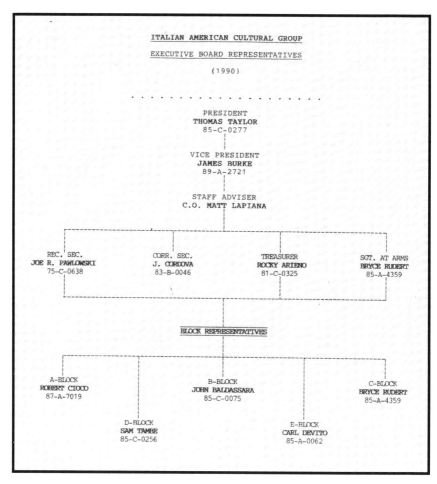

Attica State Prison Italian American League Executive Board. There were five cell blocks in Attica Prison. Each block had its own representative on the board. In 1990, Thomas Taylor took over control of the Italian American League Executive Board and made Jimmy Burke his Vice-president. Jimmy Burk was the mobster made famous in the movie "Goodfellas." He headed the crew that committed the Lufthansa Heist in New York City.

Italian American Festival. Thomas Taylor is second from right.

Italian American Festival, from left to right, are Louie Pascolini, Buffalo; Jimmy Roberts, Rochester; Tom Taylor, Rochester; Marco Cirreo, New York City, Pizza Connection, and Tommy Lauri from New York City.

After a few years of good behavior I was placed in Honor Block where we had access to telephones, stoves and refrigerators. And that worked out swell for a few more years until some Rat Bastard dropped a tab to the superintendent's office with this detailed letter.

I am writing this letter because I am disgusted at the corruption at Attica Correctional facility.

In the Package Room you have several inmates who are running a minor racket along with, and possibly for, the guards. Inmates JOHN SATIRO and Joseph STACIONE collect cigarettes from other inmates so special articles and extra packages are allowed in (Marlboros to be exact). CO'S POZ and SWEENY are paid off with cigarettes. I know this is true because I paid POZ cigarettes myself. STACIONE and SATIRO get several packages per month sent to them. Other inmates have them sent to them and they pay the guards and then they (the inmates) split or are paid off. This can easily be checked by the log at the front gate.

Check these inmates' cells. Look at the foodstuff in 46 Company's refrigerator. You will find a lot of raw meat. STACIONE just came back from a family reunion visit. His family brings up whatever contraband he wants. Its already worked out at the Package Room as to what he'll get and they'll get. The food is brought in as if its for the FRP. SATIRO carries it back and keeps it in the 46 Company fridge and freezers which is why there is never any room for the other inmates' stuff.

The Italians have both refrigerators jammed full with their stuff. SAL LOMBARDI, VINNIE and SAL LAVACCO plus several other Italians, including Mike (works in the Law Library) all chip in and feed CO McDONALD (2nd floor Day Officer) so he keeps quiet. These white guys run the second floor through CO McDONALD. The Italians get the choice cells on the 2nd floor in Honor Block.

Inmate Sal LOVACCO works in the Reception Building where he is allowed by CO KALASH to steal and sell stolen property from incoming inmates. Check these guys' cells for contraband, FANS, TYPEWRITERS. RADIOS, CASSETTES and PLAYERS that were stolen from incoming inmates. They all have table model fans, radios etc. Permits are easy to obtain. JOHN SATIRO works with the guards in the Package Room. Check STACIONE'S cell. His typewriter has 75,000 memory, which isn't allowed. Sex offenders are either run off the 2nd floor in Honor Block or forced to stay on waiting lists until single cells open up.

EARL TONEY, (44 Company) the Visiting Room Photographer, is a drug runner. From his job he isn't watched as much as the visitors, so he brings back drugs and passes them out 44 Companies windows to A Block inmates. TONEY also passes out weapons to his fellow Blood buddies through the A Block window. I am sure a lot of razor blades have been found in A Block over the past year. Check his cell and look at the stolen shirts and shoes. Shoes are often altered.

I almost forgot, the stuff that is stolen in the reception building by LOVACCO is brought back to Honor Block by the plumber and the electricians in their workboxes (carried by inmates electrician VIZZINI and plumber PETE.

There is plenty more but you will have to get one of the guys mentioned to crack and they can give you the full low-down of the operation. Inmates TOMMY TAYLOR and AL VICTORY are the money behind part of this operation. I know all the people involved are making pretty good money from this.

You'll have to use special officers when you search as a lot of the officers are paid by the inmates to cover for them. I know that there are a lot of drugs involved but these are kept very low key with the Spanish guys through TONEY. I also think VICTORY has a hand in this operation.

THIS IS ALL TRUE ALL YOU HAVE TO DO IS LOOK AND YOU WILL SEE FOR YOURSELF.

RECEIVEI

JUL 0 7 1999

ATTICA CORR. FACILIT
SUPERINTENDENT'S OFF:

They hit our cells at 5 a.m. in the morning and within two hours we were on our way to different prisons. I wound up in Comstock Correctional Facility. It was one of the worst places to do time, especially if you did not have anyone on the outside that you could reach out to in times of need. I was fortunate in that area.

Legalwise, I was being represented by another of Rochester's finest lawyers, author of "The Hammer Conspiracies," Frank Aloi. He handled my conviction before the United States Court and the Supreme Court of Appeals and we almost got the reversal.

Once these facilities know that you are in contact with an attorney and family members they are hesitant to mistreat you medical wise or otherwise. I was there almost six months before I was able to return to a facility closer to home.

Salvatore 'Sammy G' Gingello

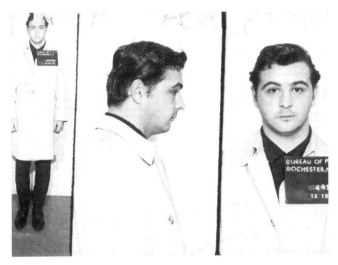

Salvatore "Sammy G" Gingello

Sammy was my "rabbi." When we were young men, Sam was a Teamster in the Teamsters Union and I was a laborer in the Laborer's Union.

We both worked on the same job in the Town of Gates, N.Y. for an out of town construction company. Sam had his own little red truck on the job. We were both young guys in our early twenties.

One of the watering holes on the East side that we frequented for girls and drinks was called The Garden Grill. We went to Skinny's for clams. So I was in the Grill one night, Sam was on the other end of the bar arguing with a couple of guys. I saw that and went right over there. As soon as I got there, Sam grabbed one of the guys by the front of his shirt and I grabbed the other guy. I looked over at Sam and said, "What do you want to do with them?"

"Throw them the fuck out of here," Sam replied.

We walked the two guys to the front door. As we were throwing them out, Sam was yelling at them, "If you come back, you will be sorry." When we get back to the bar Sam asks me, curiously, breaking the silence, "You don't want to know what that was about?"

"No Sam, there was two of them and only one of you. Not that you couldn't have taken them both," I said.

With a smile, he laughed. He never did say what that beef was about, but right up until he died that was our private joke, on the Tripp job.

Every once in a while he would stop by me with that little red truck and say, "Are you ready to know what that beef was about," and we'd laugh.

.

My First Felony

On another occasion a similar incident happened. That's where I got my first felony, which made me a second felony offender when the case with Morganti and Mancuso came up.

We were getting a lot of overtime on the job. After work we would stop in a saloon for some cold beers. So we stopped in a place called "Charlie Vella's," a club near the mall in Greece, N.Y. My brother Dick worked on the job with me and there was three or four company men in the bar also.

One of the guys was a real bully who was picking on a smaller guy that worked with me. So I said to him,

"Why don't you pick on someone your own size."

"**Like you,**" he says.

"**Yea, like me,**" I said, and we started going at it. Someone called the cops right away as they were there in minutes. Of course the cop came right to me. Officer Leslie Simmons was his name.

"**What's the problem,**" he says to me.

"**No problem,**" I replied.

"**Well, judging by the spilled drinks on the floor it looks like there was one and you were pointed out as being the trouble maker, so you can leave,**" the officer said to me.

"**I just bought this drink,**" I replied. So if I can be reimbursed for it, I will leave," I said.

The cop said, "**You're leaving now**" as he grabbed me by the arm.

I turned around on the barstool and without thinking, I hit him with a short right hook. Damn, he went flying. It is not a felony to hit a cop unless you are under arrest. So the lying S.O.B. claimed he said "You're under arrest," to me.

A witness said at the trial that the officer pulled his gun out and I kicked it, the gun, out of the officer's hand as the gun cleared the holster. I don't remember that at all. I remember someone putting me in a full nelson. Looking into the mirror behind the bar, it was a State Trooper, Meyering was his name. I couldn't move.

While looking into the mirror I also saw my brother running the length of the bar with a stool over his head. He slammed the stool on the troopers head and shoulders, dropping him to the floor like a sack of potatoes.

I told my brother to go out the back door and I went out the front. He got away and I ran into the posse. So they got me down at the station booking me, and in comes my brother, yawning.

"**I understand my brother's been arrested for intox, what's his bail,**" my brother asked.

"**There's the other one,**" a cop yelled. So, we both ended up on trial for assault. The jury's verdict was "not guilty" for my brother, but they returned a "guilty" verdict for me. I wound up with five years probation.

John "Broadway" Cavagrotti disappeared on Sept. 21, 1967.

Okay, the years go by and I wound up in Attica for nine years. When I get out, Sam's the "Man." I had running consecutively with my seven and 1/2 to 12 year sentence, two one year sentences running wild with each other for assaulting two sheriffs in the county jail. After serving my extortion sentence in Attica, I began my time in the county jail.

When I was in the Monroe County Jail, Sam was also there, serving a year, I think, for buying stolen property, leather coats, from Zeke Zimmerman. Oskie DeMarco was also in there, and Snuffy Grock too.

Snuffy was "Broadway" Cavagrotti's partner in the gambling joint when Broadway disappeared. After that Sam became Snuffy's partner. So Sam's conviction was perhaps for gambling, since Snuffy and Oskie's convictions were gambling convictions.

**Frank Valenti
Rochester Mafia "Boss"
from 1964-1972**

Frank Valenti was also in there. Valenti told me to go see his brother Stanley when I got out and to tell him "Frank sent me." Which I didn't do. He also had John Reial as his bodyguard. Reial worked for Gus Genivolla, the Sausage man.

Snuffy was Sam's partner and years prior he had given up ticker tape machines in the city, and who had them, Sam! So this Reial was calling him a rat, so I end up punching him out. After I first confronted him, he looked at me and said, **"I'll say whatever I want to say."**

Well he didn't say it any more.

We were all out on work release, me, Sam, Oskie and Snuffy. I was working for Bob Dimeno, and of course it was a "no show" job. Sam told me to go down to the Toigary Shirt Shop on Main Street, introduce myself to the guy, and buy a half dozen shirts, which I did.

One week later I had a court date where my two one year sentences were reviewed and modified to run concurrently (at the same time) instead of consecutively, and time served! Jokingly, I say to Sam, "What would have happened if I bought twelve shirts?"

"Sammy G" Gets Cheated

Danny Paulino, Charlie Russo, and Pauly Comfort had a crap game on Portland Avenue. They were using loaded dice in the game that Paulino had brought in from Buffalo. "Sammy G" stopped in early, played for a while, and lost a few thousand dollars!

After he left, one of the spots fell off one of the dice. Someone saw it but did not say anything right then. But word got back to Sammy. That evening, Dick Marino's son was getting married. The reception was at Stauffer's Party Room on the top floor.

Sam got me and Billy Barton to hold the elevator. He says not to let anyone on it until he comes with Charlie Russo. When they get on the elevator and the doors shut, Sam wanted Charlie to start catching a beating right to the ground floor.

When the elevator opened they had to call an ambulance for Charlie, who was taken to the hospital for treatment. Danny Paulino left town. Bobby Comfort called me to help his brother Paulie, which I did. I told Sam that Paulie wanted to give the money back to Sam, the money he lost on the crooked dice table; but he was outvoted, 2 to 1. Those guys thought they would be in worse trouble if they admitted to running a crooked game.

Charles Russo brother of Jake Russo (50)

So Sam says, **"Tell Paulie he's got a pass."** Sam continued, **"Get word to Paulino that if he comes back to town, he's dead!"**

Then Sam went over to see Murph Russo, Charlie's brother. Sam tells Murph that if Charlie wasn't his (Murph's) brother, he would be dead; not for the money, but for the disrespect!

Joey Tiraborelli

Joey Tiraborelli, step-son of Rochester Mafia "Boss" Samuel Russotti

Before the start of the A and B conflict, I was in the Centurion Bar one night with Freddie Pellicone and G.I. Joe. I was having a pretty good time and dancing with a girl. When I left the dance floor and returned to the bar I saw G.I arguing with Joey Tiraborelli, who thinks he's untouchable.

Anyhow, I try to diffuse the situation by stepping in between them, saying, "C'mon Joey, (stata zit)"

Tiraborelli yells, "Don't talk Italian to me, you're not Italian!"

Joey Tiraborelli, Georgia Durante, and Thomas Taylor at Georgia Durante's wedding. The picture was taken in 1979 after the bombing. When Joe was released from Attica we decided to keep our "beef" with each other buried, in Sam's honor. But I was the only one who honored that agreement.

Angelo Monachino, Rochester Mafia Soldier, turned informant.

You're right, I'm not; Joe Valachi and Angelo Monachino are. (Valachi and Monachino were both made Mafia members who turned informant.) The slightly veiled insult further enraged Joey as I stepped in between them to move GI out of the way and square off with Tiraborelli.

He moved quick. As soon as I took my eyes off him he slammed me with a glass goblet, breaking it along the side of my face and neck, narrowly missing my carotid artery, the doctor told me.

I grabbed him by his shirt and punched him in the face. Freddie, who was carrying my snub-nosed .38, slid me the gun and I began pistol whipping Joey in his face; then I stuck the gun in his mouth. Lucky for me, Bobby Silveri was there. He grabbed my arm saying, "No, Tommy, no."

Which brought me back to my senses, as there was an undercover cop in there. The way we found out was the next day they (police) wanted Joey to swear out assault charges on me.

Anyhow, that night I met Sammy and gave him the real story on the beef first hand so when they ran into him he'd already be aware and squash it, which he did. Of course they (Joey and his pals) weren't happy about it. Joey had over 20 some odd stitches in his forehead and I had a dozen on my neck.

Plans were already in motion to take me out. And what Sammy wanted didn't matter anymore.

Joe and Gail Sullivan

Joe Sullivan with his wife Gail

Joe Sullivan; man how I never saw that side of him is beyond me, and his wife Gail is just as sick. Her first husband, Augie Minerie, suddenly disappeared, never to be seen or heard from again.

Joe Sullivan related the story to me with a wink of his eye saying, "He was a fucking junkie anyhow."

Joe and Augie knew each other in prison and Joe got to know Gail through prison visits when she came to visit her husband, Augie.

The Rochester Mob War was going on for months. Everyone knew one another. I was an A-team member working for John Fiorino with Joe "The Hop." Tony Oliveri was insisting that we needed someone to get up close to whack a few of the idiots since they were only coming out at night, sneaking around like the Viet-Cong, with bombs!

So, "The Hop" says, "Do you know anyone?'

"Ya, I know a couple of Irish guys in New York City I will call in," I said.

"Okay," says "The Hop."

Joe "The Hop" Rossi, Rochester Mafia Captain

So, I call in Sullivan. He meets me at a restaurant, but he has Gail with him. He sends her back to the motel and we talked some business. Sullivan said he was ready for some work. So I let Sully talk with "The Hop," as "The Hop" is a captain and more or less co-signed for Sully being with us.

I told Sully I would call him in when we needed him. But before Sully went back to New York City I brought him over to the house and introduced him to my wife. I had rented a cottage out at the lake for two weeks one for my family, uncles, aunts, kids, etc.', the other week was for friends, Pelusio, GI Joe, Liam McGee, Bobby Comfort and Ray Bianchi. Torpey wasn't there. (He was never invited.)

This is an important fact. According to Louis DiGuilio's testimony, the cottage was where the conspiracy plot to kill Fiorino and "take over Rochester" was hatched between us. They (the prosecution) needed to corroborate DiGuilio's testimony since he was a participant in the crime.

Somehow they convinced Gail Sullivan to testify against us at the trial and say that Thomas Torpey was with us at the cottage. What did the government have on her that would make her lie and cooperate with them against her husband's friends?

Gail Sullivan liked to claim that she did not know about Joe's dark side in the beginning, when in fact she was his dark side. It started with her first husband, Lil Augie Minneri, who was a friend of Joe's. They were incarcerated together in State Prison.

Augie was released before Joe and he was with Gail when Joe came home (from prison). But Gail wanted to be with Joe and Joe wanted to be with Gail. So one night Joe and Augie went out for a few drinks. It is unknown whether or not Gail was with them.

But as Joe was telling me the story he looked at me and winked while he says, "Augie never made it home that night," wink, wink. He then added, "Fuck him. He was a junkie anyway." Thus started the love story between Gail and Joe Sullivan.

When Joe had a few drinks he liked to talk and brag a little bit. He was trying to impress me at the same time. So he continues and proceeded to tell me about an insurance contract he had. The guy was gay and he and his boyfriend couldn't get together because he was married. He also carried a sizable insurance policy on her (his wife).

If Joe could take care of her and make it look like an insane intruder broke into the house and did it, he would pay him when the insurance policy was settled. Of course he does not mention that or the fact that along with the guy's wife, is a six year old child. I did not find that out until the feds were looking for him after Fiorino was killed. Liam McGee came and told me, "Only a mad dog could kill two women and a child," hence the nickname "Mad Dog."

I got sick to my stomach. He said the two women and one six year old boy were all stabbed to death and had their throats slashed by an insane person, a crazy person, a psychopathic mad dog.

The weeks went by and Sullivan kept calling for his part of the policy (insurance) and they keep putting him off. So he told me that his wife Gail convinced him that they already received the money. So now, they have to pay, his dark side said.

So Sully and Gail go over to their house with a plan to either get their money or kill them. The plan was to put a handgun with a silencer on it in Gail's purse. When they got to the house Gail was supposed to put the purse on the floor between them. Joe would have a cigarette in his mouth and ask Gail where's the lighter. She would point to her purse.

That was the plan if when they got there the guy claimed he did not get the insurance money yet. And that is exactly what happened. So, as Joe bent down, presumably to obtain a lighter, he grabs the gun, stands back up and shoots the two men in the face and the head.

Both victims were knocked down and were out on the floor. Blood splattered everywhere and Joe and Gail went to the bathroom to wash off the blood. All of a sudden both victims came to, they were only temporarily knocked out! They ran out of the house and started running down the street yelling for help!

The silencer on Joe's gun was not made right. It was slightly off center, so instead of the slug coming out of the hole it came out like shrapnel. But Sullivan fancied himself to be a "hit man" and not the psychopathic serial killer that he was. He kept the gun and the useless silencer, but reflected that they work miracles in the hospital these days, bringing people back to life; so he now cuts peoples throats to make sure that they are dead.

Then Sully continued on and told me how he and Marco Tedesco had tried to kill three people that they were partying with. Actually they had gone to a stripper's apartment to buy an ounce of coke. But when they got there they just opened fire on everyone in the room.

Richard Bretz was killed along with the young stripper, Virginia Carson. Andrew "Butch" Soldo, the stripper's boyfriend was shot in the neck but survived. He identified Marko Tedesco as one of the killers, but he never identified Sullivan.

I asked Joe why he did it. Joe said that they were going to kill him and Marko, so they struck first (yeah right).

I met Tedesco in Attica while I was president of the Italian American League. He was a simple minded guy who wound up killing himself in Clinton Correctional Facility, by overdosing himself with heroin. I guess he could not live with his demons. He also knew that he would never get released from prison.

So, Joe had Gail and their two sons come to Rochester to stay at the cottage. I had a 28-foot Searay Cabin Cruiser. It slept six and had a head, a stove, shower, etc. While we were out on it Joe asked me if he can use it later to go kill this girl (Teresa Palmiere).

Theresa Palmiere

Joe told me that the girl was pregnant He was in trouble because he couldn't marry her and he did not want Gail to find out, so he figured it would be easier to just kill her. But, I'll be a son-of-a-bitch, the next time Joe came to Rochester he brought her (Theresa Palmiere) with him.

I told Joe that we did not need him right now and we would contact him when we did. We all had a ton of heat on us; especially him, since police confiscated his car after the Fiorino hit. The trunk contained Joe's whole life story, including the gun and bullshit silencer he used in his last couple of "hits."

I have no idea why he kept that gun and kept using it. Why hadn't he thrown it away? Joe fashioned himself to be a professional hit man, but he foolishly kept everything that could tie him to the previous crimes he committed. He also had pictures in the trunk of his car; pictures that were taken at my cottage.

The very first thing I did after police discovered Sully's identity was to destroy all the pictures I had that were taken at the cottage with his family, his wife and kids, etc., pictures that could link Joe Sullivan and myself together. I destroyed all of them including the ones that went back to our football days in Attica prison.

All the good that did. Louis DiGuilio, the driver in the Fiorino hit, was getting ready to flip. He was so full of shit! His stated reason for flipping was that he couldn't even get commissary money (from his co-conspirators). He got the money through his father and his lawyer, Les Bradshaw. When Louie was first busted, Charlie West went over to see him. He said Louie had been worked over pretty good.

Bobby Comfort, above, and Nicky Mastrodonato picked up Mad Dog Sullivan after the Fiorino murder, enabling Sullivan to escape.

Bobby Comfort was always with me and when Joe Sullivan got jammed, they, Bobby and Nicky Mastrodonato, came over to get him out. He was in a bar called The Boulevard Grill, at the end of the shopping center where the Blue Gardenia was located. In fact, Joe was in Nicky's house when the cops went there! The cops asked a few questions at the door and then left.

Thomas Marotta

Tom Marotta

Tom Marotta called the Blue Gardenia after Fiorino was hit. He asked them who was there and they told him I was. So he asked to talk to me.

"What happened," Marotta asked.

"What happened? I'll tell you what happened," I said. "John Fiorino came over to collect an envelope (Torpey's "vig" money) and he lost his head. We still have the envelope. Why don't you come down and get it?" I taunted.

"Yeah right," he said and he hangs up.

Thomas Torpey

Torpey wasn't paying the "vig" on his gambling joint, mostly because he was strung out on coke. He fought with us during the A&B war and was in Sammy's car with me and Sam when it was blown up, so he figured he could catch some slack for a while, especially after he found out I was not paying the "vig" on a game I ran with Billy Barton on the East Side in Messbauer's Bar. When Torpey first started having trouble, Rene and Red called a sit-down at his (Torpey's) joint.

I spoke out for Tommy (Torpey) and I was telling them how he helped against the B-team and almost lost his life with Sam. I said he is still fighting the B-team, he is just having a problem and the joint ain't doing that good.

Red Russotti says, "Whatever you got going I've got to wet my beak." (He must have seen the Godfather movie ten times.) Torpey still did not pay!

After a couple of weeks, John Fiorino came to see him (Torpey) and told him he's going to pay cause he can bleed like anyone else, and then slapped him in the face. Torpey immediately came and told me, since they were trying to make moves on me too after Sam was killed, as Sam had me with him 24/7 when he was alive.

What Happened to Omerta?

Omerta is the Italian code of silence and honor at all costs, especially in the face of questioning by the authorities. Mafia business is strictly forbidden to be discussed in front of all outsiders, beginning when one is sworn into the organization via a secret ritual.

From the time that Thomas Marotta went down into Frank Valenti's basement with Sammy G. to be sworn into the Rochester Mob, he started relating what he saw and who he saw. It was a rather serious infraction of the Organization's rules.

It had been strongly rumored for years that Thomas Marotta and Sgt. John Grande of the Rochester Police Department were related. To what degree was unknown. But the two were certainly close enough to each other to tip each other off about which gambling joints were going to get raided, when all the patrons were going to get arrested, and who was doing what.

Grande was a Sgt. in the Organized Crime Task Force and Thomas Marotta a Captain in the Rochester Mafia. They made quite a team and washed each other's backs. Consigliore Rene Piccarreto was fine with it all until Marotta and Rene had a falling out.

Rene started getting heat on some of the things he had going on. He was coming up short moneywise on others. With all the other chaos going on he probably figured that if push came to shove that Marotta might testify or dry snitch against him.

Marotta's 2002 Plea Agreement

Years later, that is exactly what Tom Marotta did. He dry snitched on his co-defendants. After being paroled for his 1984 conviction on murder and conspiracy charges Marotta was once again facing life in prison for a series of criminal acts that he had been committing since his release. He committed several felony crimes including selling cocaine, money laundering, transportation of stolen vehicles and food stamp fraud. Each of those crimes carried hefty prison sentences and were also part of a larger conspiracy, which is a separate crime.

On May 2, 2002, Tom Marotta was facing life in prison once again, he chose a plea agreement instead. In his colloquy before the judge, Marotta had to plead guilty to every charge and name each of his co-conspirators that he had committed the crimes with. One by one Marotta gave them all up.

1) Nicky Fosco $100,000 food stamp fraud. Illegal sale and conspiracy to sell food stamps.

2) Nicholas Colangelo - money laundering from drug sales and illegal gambling.

3) Tony Leonardo, famed Rochester Attorney—Money Laundering and drugs.

4) Jack Russo, Anthony D'Agostino - Interstate Transportation of Stolen Motor Vehicles.

5) Joseph Iacobacci - Food Stamp Fraud, Illegal buying and selling of food stamps.

This is called "dry snitching." Thomas Marotta named each of his co-conspirators but he did not have to testify against them. But unfortunately for them, Marotta's plea agreement got each of the men named above indicted for the particular crime named.

Thomas Marotta, who was facing life in prison plus the parole time that he owed, miraculously worked out a rather favorable plea agreement. For his cooperation Marotta was sentenced to only nine years. Further, his sentence was to run concurrently (at the same time) with the parole time that he already owed. He also got to serve that time in McKean Federal Correction Facility near Bradford, PA. McKean was a medium security prison. That was a pretty sweet deal Marotta worked out without having to ever testify.

It would seem that Rene Piccarreto was right when he tried to have Marotta "hit" by Taddeo years earlier. Taddeo shot Marotta on two separate occasions on Piccarreto's orders. Why was the murder of Thomas Marotta ordered by his own boss if they didn't suspect him of "snitching"?

Rene Piccarreto

Rene Piccarreto

But what about Rene? For years everyone wondered what happened to Jake Russo, the Rochester Mafia Boss who disappeared in October of 1964. Then when Rene Piccarreto was released from prison in 2007 and living in California, he made a film of a man with a blocked out image and altered voice detailing what happened to Jake Russo.

The story goes that Stephano Magaddino, Boss of the Buffalo/Niagara Falls Mafia ordered Frank Valenti to make Jake Russo disappear for good when Valenti returned to Rochester. According to Rene, Frank Valenti invited Jake Russo to dinner at his downtown restaurant called the Quill Room. At some point Russo was taken into the basement where a couple of guys were waiting and he was strangled to death, wrapped up, and buried in an unknown location.

So much for the Italian code of Omerta!

What was the purpose of the disclosure?

Rene Piccarreto was also the recruiter of Dominic Taddeo, the A-Team hitman. Taddeo's father was a painter who worked for Rene. At that time, Dominic Taddeo was known only as a car thief, nothing more. But he turned out to be a lot more!

One day Dominic Taddeo came bursting into one of the clubs where some Mob guys where hanging out and said out loud, "I want to join your club. How do I join? I can do some work for you."

Despite this odd verbal outburst displaying his desire to join a secret organization, Dominic Taddeo was indeed hired by Rene Piccarreto to "do some work." Piccarreto gave Taddeo a hit list of C-Team members that were involved in the murder of John Fiorino, with instructions that all were to be killed.

Taddeo turned out to be a natural. Without any prior arms training he was a pretty good shot with a .45 caliber pistol. He was able to hit and kill two of his targets while driving a stolen vehicle and shooting out of the passenger side window. Both targets were suspected C-Team members. It is very unusual for one man to be both the shooter and the driver. Taddeo's third victim was a man named Nicky Mastrodonato, whom he knew. Mastrodonato was shot inside of his coin store.

Two separate attempts were made on the life of Rochester Mafia Captain, Thomas Marotta. Taddeo shot Marotta twice, hitting him several times on each occasion. Marotta survived both shootings. At first police attributed the shootings to the C-Team. But Dominic Taddeo was eventually caught and he confessed to all the shootings, the three murders, and both attempted murders of Marotta.

During Taddeo's confession he admitted that he committed the murders for Rene Piccarreto and was paid $500. Despite Taddeo's confession, Rene Piccarreto was never charged under Section 20 for Conspiracy. During sentencing, Judge Telesca made reference to Taddeo attempting to kill both Bobby Comfort and Thomas Taylor as well.

Sammy G's Trial

During Sammy's trial I testified for him. At the job where I was working, Jimmy Massaro was the foreman. We worked for InSanna Construction, laying pipe and installing sewers in Webster. Angelo Monachino was Superintendent.

So, the district attorney was trying to make me look like an interested witness (knowing all the mob guys). He asked me how well I knew Red Russotti. My answer was, "I know him like I know you. I know who you are but neither one of you would have me over to your house for Sunday dinner."

Anthony Malsegna

Then comes Anthony Malsegna, a (49) Monroe County Sherriff's Deputy. Malsegna claimed that he was in Tommy's joint, undercover, and he observed in the back corner, sitting at a dark table and talking in a clandestine manner were Sam Gingello, Rene Piccarreto, Sam Russotti and Tom Taylor.

I, allegedly, was the first one to leave and when I did, I stood up and I hugged and kissed everyone on the cheek, according to Malsegna. Anthony Malsegna's statement got me indicted for perjury.

But that conviction was later dismissed, along with the other convictions of Sam and the other guys once one of the sheriff's deputies was "dipped in the river Jordon" and began confessing to all the fabricated evidence that the police manufactured in order to get convictions. I was one of them, I was convicted of perjury, using perjured testimony.

On Oct. 1, 1979, The United States Court of Appeals Second Circuit reversed my conviction based on the fact that the Monroe County District Attorney's Office knowingly used perjured testimony against me. I had already served a year in prison.

Split With Billy Barton

William "Billy" Barton

Billy Barton and I went way back. We had been friends for a long time and we worked on many jobs together. So, what caused the split between myself and Billy, pushing Barton to end up on the B-Team with Tommy DiDio and Sonny Celestino? Didio had told him (Barton) that I wasn't paying the "vig" on our gambling joint. So Barton felt that I was cheating him. He never took into account that I was paying all the utilities, the rent, and the refreshments too.

I explained it all to him, but he still didn't get it. But what do you expect from a guy with a fifth grade education? Such a lame excuse to switch sides and go over with DiDio. I met Barton in person at the Blue Gardenia and asked him how he could turn against me and Sammy.

"I'm going where the money is Tom," Barton told me.

"Ahhh, yes," I said, "For a handful of silver you're gonna jump sides?"

Barton replied, "You'd be smart to come with me because Sammy and them guys aren't coming out, ever! They will die in there."

"We'll see," I said. "I think they are going to get a reversal."

Lo and behold, 14 months later they got a reversal and their convictions were set aside.

The 44 Club Incident

Okay, Sammy is dead. I am beefing with the Mob! They've tried to set me up a half dozen different ways. So, I am used to the way they are treating Torpey and I decide to side with him because it's just a matter of time before it's me. I had pulled Sullivan in to off Fiorino; I had 24 hour 7 day a week surveillance.

It was about 8 p.m. Myself, Torpey, Tom and his brother, Mike Pelusio, were out cruising around the city. Asshole Rene Piccarreto had been sending threats out about what he is going to do to Pelusio.

We stopped in front of the 44 Club on Lake Avenue and we all go inside, pushing the doorman out of the way on our way in. Once we were inside there was a blackjack game in progress with several people. Charlie Russo was running it for Moe Alaimo. They had to pay the A-team the "vig."

Charlie was Jake Russo's brother. Jake had been in charge of the Mob, but he fell out of favor and "disappeared," and was presumed dead. *

---

* Jake Russo was last seen in October of 1964. A recent 2018 story emerged and was told to Democrat and Chronicle Newspaper Investigative Journalist Gary Craig by Loren Piccarreto, a made Rochester Mafia member, who at one time held the position of "Acting Underboss" in that organization.

The story was an explanation of what happened to Jake Russo. According to Loren, Rene, his father, had a tape recording describing exactly what happened to him (Russo). As the story goes, the Russo's were responsible for making sure that Buffalo, Stephano Magaddino specifically, was getting his cut of Rochester's gambling profits. Allegedly Russo had claimed poverty and Magaddino had him killed for not kicking up an additional $500 per week.

So I sit down at the blackjack table and Charlie looks at me and says, "Are you playing?" I just looked at Charlie and said, "You dirty motherfucker, they killed your brother and you had Rene stand up at your wedding?"

"I know," he says, as he gives me a pitiful look.

So, I backhanded him so hard he fell off his chair. "Give that to Rene for me," I said. "And tell him to stop threatening my friends." As I do that, Mike Pelusio knocks Moe Alaimo down and Torpey starts kicking him with his cowboy boots. Alaimo screams like a little bitch, "I'm going to tell blue eyes" (Tom Marotta).

So, I reached in my pocket for a handful of change as I grabbed Alaimo by the back of the neck, ordering him to open his mouth as I shoved the change in. Tell Marotta we'll be down at the Town Square. (The Town Square was a bar on Lake Avenue.)

Marotta doesn't show, but John Grande's crew does. John Grande (51) was to Tom Marotta like John Connelly was to Whitey Bulger of Boston! That is why Rene had him shot twice to no avail., for their tit for tat!

John Grande

Myself and the two Pelusio's were charged with 2nd degree assault. Alaimo put Torpey's cowboy boots on me, claiming I was the one kicking him in the ribs, probably on Marotta's orders. When I played football in Attica Prison I kicked field goals. If I was kicking Alaimo with cowboy boots on, every one of his ribs would have been broken. Of course we went to trial and were convicted.

They all testified except Charlie Russo. He appeared before the grand Jury and secured the indictment, but the district attorney did not put Charlie on the witness stand at the trial. He probably figured it would not be worth taking the chance of cross-examination, considering the Russo Crime Family background.

Loansharking / (Sammy G) Gets Blown Up

Sammy gave me loansharking on the East Side. There was a gambling joint on Portland Avenue. Guys going broke from gambling could get a loan, 6 for 5. I had brought Tony Oliveri in. The war was still going on. I had recruited Tony when we were in the joint. When Sam came home he made Tony a Teamster. But, Sam didn't trust him 100 percent. *

I started a $15,000 bank and was doing pretty good with it. But we were right in the middle of the A & B Mob War. **"I had 24-hour surveillance on me. No matter where I went, I had it on me."** I used to tell Sammy, They're our own body guards. Nobody is going to make a move on us with the cops watching us. They carry guns legally and everything.

We were used to having the police follow us everywhere. But that morning was different. There was no surveillance that night. I usually drove. But, at the restaurant we argued over whether or not we should check beneath the Buick for explosives. I wanted to check for bombs, but Sammy thought it was a sign of weakness. The Mob War had been going on for months. The B-Team was bombing everything, but they never got anybody.

When we got to the car after leaving the restaurant Sammy insisted on driving. Sammy and I had met years previously on a construction job. Sammy used to be a Union Dump truck driver and I was the laborer. So Sammy jokingly says to me, give me the keys, I'm the Teamster. You can't touch anything with wheels on it.

*As it turned out Sammy G. was right about Anthony Oliveri. He turned out to be a government informant who testified against Rene Piccarreto at the Federal trial. Oliveri in his debriefing had also involved me, claiming that I picked him up after the DiDio murder. Oliveri was one of many Rochester Mobsters who entered into the Federal Witness Protection Program.

Seconds after we entered the car, Gingello in the driver's seat, me in the passenger seat and Torpey in the back, the Buick burst into flames.

The inside of Sammy G's car following the explosion. Sammy was sitting in the driver's seat that night. I was sitting in the passenger seat.

The ATF guy told me that what had saved me was the transmission. In that year, the 1978 Buick Park Avenue's transmission plate was extra thick for some reason. So the force of the blast went to the point of least resistance, which was downward into the parking lot and then upwards into the car.

The impact of the bomb tore off one of Sammy's legs and the other leg was left hanging by the tendons as his torso slumped down and out of the car when the door blew open. I never heard the blast. It felt like somebody smashed me across the feet with a flat board. The force of the impact blew my left shoe off my foot, traveling through the roof of the car, landing a football field away. I knew something happened. I knew enough to get out of the car. As I opened the door to get out, I simultaneously reached over to pull Sam out too.

His seat was empty, and as I reached for him I felt a warm, wet sensation from all the blood.

I got out of the car stumbling around. I was in shock! I heard Torpey yelling and cussing. Tommy Izzo, who owned the nightclub we just left, came running out and up to me, slowly taking me off my feet as he covered me with a couple of coats. He started asking me questions that I had no idea of what the answers were.

Sam knew these cockroaches had bombs and he knew that they were using them! Some time prior to being blown up at Tommy's (Izzo's), Sam and John Fiorino were going in the Blue Gardenia one day and a bomb was hidden in a snow bank at the entrance to the restaurant, as they walked through the pathway, it was detonated!

Fortunately, the explosion was not close enough to harm them. They both got back in the car and went to John's house and called me. I went right over and convinced Sam to go back to the Blue, showing them all that he was okay. and that he was not frightened by that bullshit. When in fact we were!

We were supposed to take every precaution possible not to expose ourselves like that again. That's why I could never understand Sam's thinking about not looking under the car. It cost him his life that night and almost mine.

Tommy Izzo squeezed my shoulder to get my attention, and told me, "Don't worry Tommy, I gotcha." He had a gun stuck in his waistband keeping people away from me and he stayed with me until they put me in the ambulance.

Looking back, that's some friend willing to come out and jump in the middle of that car bombing to help us. His help didn't stop there as I will relate later as this low life piece of crude "Sonny Celestino," who placed the bomb under the car, should not even have been alive and the person who saved his life at the time was Sammy G!

Dominic (Sonny) Celestino

Dominic "Sonny" Celestino

Sonny Celestino had violated one of the Mob's rules about not messing around with another member's wife.

William "Billy" Barton and I were both on the A-team for many years. We were each others wingman and we did some heavy work together, but I won't get in to that. Billy calls me one day and says, "Gotta see you Tommy, we got some work."

So I meet Billy and he says he has the contract for us to hit Sonny Celestino! Apparently, Sonny was messing around with Eddie Kramer's wife. Eddie was a strong "Associate" of the Mob, but not made. (73)

Joe Trieste, Tommy Marotta, Ben Manning (owner of the Blue Gardenia), and Ed Kramer.

"That's where the problem is Billy," I told him. Continuing on, I said, "Sonny is made. You know yourself we would need the okay before we moved on him."

Billy says, "Who's going to know?"

"I'm not going to disrespect Sammy like that. If we're going to do it, it's going to be done right," I said.

So I took Billy down with me to go see Sammy G. After I laid it out for him, Sammy says to me, "Tommy, this is why I love you, you do everything right. I'll take care of this," he said.

Sam did take care of it. He called a "sit-down" with all involved and he confronted Celestino after verifying the allegation. Instead of okaying the hit, Sam went easy on Sonny and he used the infraction of Mob rules to run Celestino out of the Mob. Now if Sam had given Billy and I the okay to whack Celestino, he would not have been around to put the bomb under Sammy's car!

'Sammy G' Gets Blown Up (cont.)

The ambulance brought me to the hospital, that's where I found out that Sammy didn't make it. That really hurt me, more than the bomb!

I started yelling that I wanted out of the hospital, saying that, "I'm leaving come, hell or high water." I was afraid that they were going to shoot me up with sodium pentitol (truth serum). I wanted to get back out on the street and have a go at the scumbags we were fighting.

I was told that when Sam temporarily regained consciousness and saw that he had no legs and saw all the intravenous tubing in his arm, that he reached over and pulled them all out while giving the room full of onlookers the bird! And then he passed away. Someone in the room took a picture of him.

Well, that was just a bunch of urban folklore. Those things never happened. I spoke to the doctor who told me there was no way he could have survived. He was too far gone in shock to pull through.

Damn! Talk about divine intervention. I had been driving for Sam since he came home (from prison). That night Sam insisted on driving himself, without me looking under the car. The other strange thing was for some unknown reason we did not have a tail on us that night. We always had a tail on us. But not that night.

I never gave it much thought, conspiracy wise, until Tommy Izzo told me one day that right after the explosion, Bill Mahoney was standing right in front of Eddie's Chop House down the street on Main Street.

The Mahoney Connection

William Mahoney

William "Backroom Bill" Mahoney was the Chief of Detectives when he was put in jail, stripping him of his position along with three detectives under him for manufacturing false evidence against Sammy and others in order to gain a conviction for murder and conspiracy charges. Sammy wound up in prison for 14 months as a result of the police corruption.

Detective Anthony Malsegna was one of those officers. Mahoney was in the Monroe County Jail when I was there. His nickname at headquarters was "Backroom Bill." He had a reputation for taking innocent prisoners into the "backroom" where he would beat confessions out of them.

A couple of his bullshit "confessions" were set aside by Appellate Courts and large settlements were awarded to defendants who had confessed under duress.

Mahoney was partners with William "Billy" Lupo (Rochester Mafia Capo) in the Renaissance Massage Parlor and his bookmaking operation. Lupo wound up with a couple of holes in his head for allegedly stealing money from Sammy G's house, money that was supposed to go to Las Vegas.

William "Billy" Lupo, Rochester Mafia Capo

Lupo's death caused Mahoney to lose his half of the "take" (illicit money) from Lupo's operations. Mahoney always blamed Sam for that but he

Detective Anthony Malsegna, Rene Piccarreto and Chief of Detectives William Mahoney

could not do anything about it, legally. But from that moment on Mahoney had it in for Sam. He would do everything in his power to get him.

As Chief of Detectives of the Monroe County Detective Bureau, Mahoney was able to find several detectives who were willing to fabricate surveillance notes and then testify to the manufactured evidence at murder and conspiracy trials. The false evidence led to murder convictions and imprisonment, which ultimately facilitated the beginning of the Rochester Mob Wars.

Before they went away, I stopped over at the County Jail to see Sam. I had testified for him at the trial. The same trial where Malsegna falsely testified that he observed me embracing Sam, Rene, and Red, prior to leaving Ben's Café and prior to my testifying.

When Sam came home I was with him 24/7, driving anywhere he wanted to go. Bobby Silveri had bought Sam a 1978 Buick Park Avenue. We went to Buffalo to have a "sit-down" with Russell Buffalino. It was Sam, Red, Rene, and myself. We met in a club called The Gold Coast.

They were all seated at a table and I was at the bar nearby. I noticed that when Buffalino spoke, he looked directly at Sam 95 percent of the time. Sammy was putting things together, and with Buffalino's okay, we would be off and running.

So we went to Florida. Then when we returned to Rochester, Sam started getting into the vending machine business-jukebox, cigarette machines, etc.

Florida

Several years prior, I had a physical confrontation with a doctor at Strong Memorial Hospital over my daughter, and the doctor ended up with a broken ear drum. Just before the statute of limitations was about to expire on that incident, Sam was tipped off that they were going to arrest me for that.

So Sam tells me to get a hold of "Bow Wow" (John Fiorino's street name).

"I want you and him to go to Florida and check out some clubs. We're moving down there to get something going. Plus by the time you get back, the statute of limitations will have run out with the doctor," says Sam.

So John and I went down to Florida. First we had to go to a hotel and report to Joe "Lead Pipe Joe" Todaro, Buffalo Mob Boss. They owned the hotel. We had to let them know we were in town. When we got there he was at the pool with Big Al LaMonica, who I knew well from the joint (Attica).

That impressed John, as he did not know that I knew the Buffalo crew like that. Al was later whacked by a guy named Dilly Spadarrow over money.

So we go to the house we have in Miami. The next day we meet the realtor and we checked out a couple of clubs. That night we went to a couple of spots to see what kind of business they had. One of those clubs was called the "Lime Liter."

Then we went to another club named "Forties." There was a gal there in her late thirties with a couple of real hot young ladies in their early twenties. I struck up a conversation with the older gal while John was trying like hell to pull one of the younger ones.

Once I found out what she did, business wise, she had my undivided attention. She had her own bonding, bail and insurance business. She was able to bond in Florida, New York, New Jersey, etc. We hit it off and made a night of it. I brought her home with us, much to John's disdain.

We had breakfast the next morning and she left me her phone numbers and other contact information. Her name was Beansy. On the way home John kept breaking my balls that she and I were going to have little kosher beaners!

Anyhow when we got home we met with Sam, filling him in on everything, specifically mentioning the joints that he may be interested in. In my report to Sammy I included Beansy and explained to Sam that she would insure anything we wanted insured and she could get anyone out on bail.

John starts laughing out loud. I looked at him and said, "The joke will be on you buddy when she starts getting us out on bail."

John answered, "Ya Right! We will need her over my dead body!"

A Monroe County Medical Examiners crew removes the body of John Fiorino outside of the Blue Gardenia.

Well, there lays John, dead in front of the Blue Gardenia. Months later I was charged with calling "Mad Dog" in from New York to have him killed, after he slapped Torpey in the face while telling him he could bleed like anyone else, unless he paid.

Louis DiGuilio

The whole story was told by Louis DiGuilio. Torpey's bail was set at $200,000 and mine was $500,000. I was able to retain one of the best lawyers in New York State, John Speranza. He was able to get me another bail hearing and had my bail reduced down from 500,000 to $200,000, that's what Torpey's was.

But then the local bondman wouldn't touch it. His reason? "Afraid I'll wind up in a fifty gallon drum," he said.

But we all know that the local bondsman and police work together at times, and this was one of those times. So the call went down to Beansy in Florida and she was more than willing to make arrangements for my bail and release.

$500,000 Bail for Taylor

On **June 15, 1982**, a bail hearing was held for Thomas Taylor who stood accused of hiring Joseph Sullivan to kill John Fiorino. Judge Eugene Bergin set bail at $500,000. Earlier that month Bergin had set the same bail for Thomas Torpey, who was Taylor's co-conspirator and co-defendant. (54)

$500,000 bail for Taylor

Bail has been set at $500,000 cash or property for Thomas E. Taylor, reputed underworld figure accused of murder in the shotgun slaying of John N. Fiorino outside the Blue Gardenia restaurant in Rochester last year.

Taylor and another reputed organized crime figure, Thomas M. Torpey, are accused of hiring contract killer Joseph John Sullivan to kill Fiorino as a warning to another mob faction.

Monroe County Court Judge Eugene W. Bergin set bail earlier this month at $500,000 for Torpey and held a bail hearing June 15 for Taylor. Defense lawyer John Speranza told Bergin $500,000 bail was unreasonable and argued that Taylor is a life-long Rochester-area resident with family and business ties here.

Bergin yesterday announced his decision to accept Assistant Monroe County District Attorney Donald J. Wisner's recommendation of $500,000. Bergin said he was influenced by Taylor's past record, which includes a 1973 parole violation when he fled to Texas and Syracuse.

Sullivan, who is charged with murder and attempted murder, is scheduled to appear before Bergin today.

July 2, 1982
Democrat & Chronicle

John Fiorino

When I walked out, I thought back again to what John Fiorino had said to me at the meeting with him and Sam after our return from Florida in reference to needing Beansy, the Bond woman. John's exact words were, "Ya right, over my dead body."

John Fiorino, Rochester Mafia Captain

John Fiorino was Vice-President of Teamsters Local #398 in Rochester, N. Y. He was murdered on Dec. 17, 1981 outside of the Blue Gardenia Restaurant in Irondequoit, N.Y. by Joseph "Mad Dog" Sullivan, and on the orders of "C-Team" Mafia leaders Thomas Torpey and Thomas Taylor.

At the time of his death, The FBI considered John Fiorino to have been a "made" member and "Captain" of the Rochester Mafia Crime Family. John Fiorino had also allegedly become an informant and was cooperating with the U.S. Organized Crime Strike Force at the time of his death, although it remained undetermined whether Fiorino actually testified before he died.

If only he knew then just how right he was!

We had no idea that John had flipped with the feds. Although one night at the bar he made an observation that if anyone flipped with the feds they would only have to relocate them to Dansville.

Right about that time we were standing in front of the joint on Lyell Avenue. It was myself, Torpey, etc., John Grande stopped by. John was with the Organized Crime Task Force. We were making wisecracks back and forth and all of a sudden he says, on the level, **"We don't need any informants because we have a Mob 'Captain' cooperating."**

I remember thinking at the time, why would he say that and risk jeopardizing whoever it was? Unless that was his intention. It was possible that the connection between him and Tom Marotta would be exposed.

It was strongly rumored that they were cousins (Grande and Marotta). Marotta would slip Grande information on the opposition, like us. For instance, on the 44 Club assault on Moe Alaimo, when we left there Moe called Marotta and Marotta called Grande. He filled him in on what happened and where we were at the Town Square bar, but not to arrest Tom Torpey. (I didn't put that connection together until later.)

Victim was informant

John M. Fiorino, who was shot to death last night in what police believe was a gangland slaying, was vice president of Teamsters Local 398.

The union has been a target of a major federal grand jury investigation of Mafia activities in Rochester. Sources said Fiorino had recently turned informant, making him the third, and most powerful, organized crime figure known to be cooperating with the U.S. Organized Crime Strike Force in the probe.

The other two known informants are Anthony F. Oliveri, a reputed Mafia strongman...

Dec. 18, 1981
Democrat & Chronicle

Whitey Bulger had the Federal Agent John Connelly with basically the same agreement as did Gaspipe Casso, with the two New York City detectives doing hits for the Mob. Rene Piccarreto was fine with all this until there came a time that he and Marotta had a falling out, due to Marotta making moves on his own without sharing the proceeds.

FBI agent refuses to say if Fiorino was an informant

Defense puts the question to him in 11 different ways

By David Galante
Democrat and Chronicle

An FBI agent who testified yesterday in the

Dec. 1, 1983
Democrat & Chronicle

Dominick Taddeo

Dominick Taddeo
"Hit-man"

Thus Dominick Taddeo entered the picture, making two unsuccessful attempts at eliminating Marotta. When Taddeo was sentenced in federal court, I noticed that Tom Torpey did not appear on Taddeo's "to kill" list. Rene always said that Torpey was just a blob.

Another thing I noticed, something I picked up from Taddeo's pre-sentencing report, was that Taddeo was being paid the measly sum of $500 per hit. That is also what Joe Sullivan said he was being paid by John Sullivan in New York City (supposedly).

The only organized crime guy Sully ever got charged with killing was John Fiorino in Rochester. The other murders came to light after he was here (Rochester). Before coming to Rochester, Sullivan murdered two women and a six year old child for insurance money. Augie Minerri, Gail's first husband was shot. Sullivan also murdered a bartender and a cab driver that he thought may be able to identify him after the cab driver had picked him (Sully) up after a hit.

But Taddeo and Sullivan both said they were paid $500 per hit. You would think they would be embarrassed to admit they worked for such a small fee.

Another confession made by Taddeo was that he performed the hits at the request of Rene Piccarreto. Piccarreto was never charged. Taddeo was charged with three homicides, but there were no murder or conspiracy charges filed against the planners of the crimes.

The 'Set-ups'

Joe "The Hop" Rossi
Rochester Mafia "Captain"

Okay, so after the car bombing I am laying flat on my back at home and Joe "The Hop" and John Fiorino stopped by and asked for the shylock bank and list. I gave it to them, but it bothered me that they didn't ask me if I needed anything or if I am alright, moneywise.

The three of us were all crewed up during the A&B war. We were very close during those 14 months (when Sammy and the others were in prison). I had a bad vibe, but I couldn't quite figure out why. Once I was up and around things seemed to be okay, but not quite.

Joe the Hop called me over to his townhouse. Bobby Silveri was in there with him. They told me they were waiting for Joe Rebis to call as he was going to shoot Billy Barton. I knew Joe Rebis, and he couldn't kill an afternoon!

I was standing by the door, I came in, and I heard a noise over by the basement door and I said, "I will be right back."

As I went out the door, the Hop yelled, "Tommy, where you going?"

"I'll be right back," I said. "I forgot my cigarettes." Yeah, right, I got in the car and took off! Funny thing was the Hop never called to ask me where I went and Rebis never did shoot Billy Barton!

Samuel "Red" Russotti, Rochester Mafia "Boss" "The Boss"

Paranoid? Maybe, but I only have to be wrong once. But the next move put it together. I got a phone call from "Red" Russotti. Russotti tells me that we have trouble in Florida and he wants me to go down with him to straighten it out. Without giving it a second thought I said okay.

Russotti told me to be over to the house at 7 a.m., as he wants to get an early start. He emphasizes not to bring a gun because if we get stopped we want the car to be clean. I thought to myself, car? What, we are not flying?

Red Russotti, the Boss and I were driving to Florida? Already I did not like the sound of this. It's a 1,500 mile trip and I've always flown. During the A&B war I was a strong A-team member, with Joe "The Hop" Rossi and John "Bow Wow" Fiorino. But since Sammy's death, I noticed that my strength was diminished. I got premonitions. Sometimes I was right, sometimes I was wrong, like that time at the Hop's house.

Anyway, I got over to Red's house at 7 a.m. Talk about premonitions! How do I get out of this one? I got into the car with Red, who was the step-father of Joey Tiraborelli and two of Joey's best friends, Tommy Marotta and Joe (the pervert) LoDolce, all made members. I was the guy that put 20 something stitches in Joey's face and head.

Joey "Joey Tubes" Tiraborelli Rochester Mafia "Soldier: Step-son of "The Boss"

Sammy G. was the one who prevented retaliation being made on me. Now Sam was gone. Joe Tiraborelli had recently told me that he wanted me to drive for him when he took Rene out. It was supposed to be a wedding reception on Plank Road. Joey said he would call me and say, "Let's go fishing." and that would be the signal for me to go pick him up.

So, all of this was going through my head. We had just stopped for breakfast and I knew I had to make a move fast, as I was sure that my life depended on it. So I moaned and squirmed around in the car saying, "I have to hit the head fast, must have been something in my food that was bad." Marotta looked at Red for the o.k. With an anguished look I said, "I can't hold it!!"

So Red says, "Sure, sure, pull right in there and let Tommy out so he can go to the bathroom!" Of course Marotta came in with me, playing me close. So, I told him I have to call home and see how my daughter is. "When I left this morning, she was sick," I said (all bullshit).

So I call and my wife answers the phone, and I ask her how the baby is.

"What? I yelled, 104 temperature? Take her to the hospital immediately. I am on my way back right now."

They did their best to get me back into the car, but to no avail. They knew they lost me. Red acted like he was worried.

"Do you need any money? Do you want us to drop you off someplace, the bus station, the airport," he asked.

"No," I said. "Go take care of your business and I will meet you down there."

Everything was supposedly all straight, but as it turned out, no more was ever said about the alleged "problem" down in Florida. Right up until Sam was killed we didn't have anything going on, businesswise, in Florida.

The Cristo Collision Set-Up

I owned a classic car and I was in the process of having it restored at Cristo Collision on Ridge Road East. The car was a 1932 Lincoln KB Series, 12 cylinder. One day Gail Cristo, wife of the owner of Cristo Collision, contacted me and said she had something important to tell me. Well that was an understatement. What she told me wasn't a premonition, but it made my premonitions true.

Jimmy Cristo knew the Mob guys. They (the Mob guys) were pushing up on him to call me over to the garage at a certain pre-arranged time so they could "whack" me. Jimmy was what they called a "Strong Associate." He took care of all of the Mob's car business. He grew up with half of the guys in the Rochester Mafia and he socialized with the rest of them. So why did Jimmy's wife tip me off?

If I had to speculate I would be inclined to believe that they (the Cristo's) did not wish to be involved in a murder. Jimmy probably told his wife to tell me on the down low, which she did. Needless to say I got my car out of his garage asap.

My 1932 Lincoln KB Series, 12 cylinder.

Enter the C-Team

That was also right around the time that Torpey stopped paying the "vig" on his joint. He had developed a real bad drug habit.

As a last resort, John Fiorino was sent to collect some money from Torpey. When John's efforts were met with resistance, John slapped him in the face and told him, "You can bleed like anyone else."

I ran into Torpey right after that. We had a whole crew of guys ready to do what ever was needed.

Loren Piccarreto Rochester Mafia "Soldier" and one time "Acting Underboss"

Just prior to the above incident, Torpey had been responsible for getting Loren Piccarreto arrested. They were extorting a guy who owned a Lake Avenue bar called The Sunset Inn. There were several apartments above the bar. They were attempting to force the guy to allow them to put a massage parlor up there. But the guy ran to the cops instead and they were both busted.

"Molly" (Dick Marino) posted bail for Loren, but not for Torpey. I went and posted the $10,000 bail for Torpey, and the C-team was born.

Thomas Torpey and Thomas Taylor just getting started in Attica. From left to right are Sammy Brown from New York City, Thomas Torpey from Rochester, Eddie Cicero from Buffalo, and Thomas Taylor from Rochester.

Thomas Taylor and Marco Cirreo from The Pizza Connection.

Rochester Police Department mugshots, page one. Top left is Rochester Mafia Soldier Gene DiFrancesco. He was the triggerman in the Jimmy the Hammer Massaro murder. Bottom left is Rochester Mafia Consigliore Rene Piccarreto. Middle right is Rochester Mafia Soldier Joe Trieste.

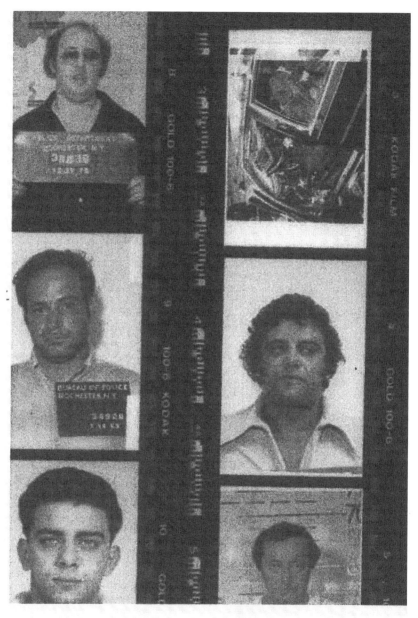

6/7/02   Mug Shots RPD copy   Page 2

Rochester Police Department mugshots, page two. Top left is Thomas "The Lion" Torpey. Middle left is Joseph LoDolce, Soldier in the Rochester Mafia. Middle right and bottom left is Rochester Mafia Captain Thomas Marotta. Bottom right is Rochester Mafia Underboss Richard Marino.

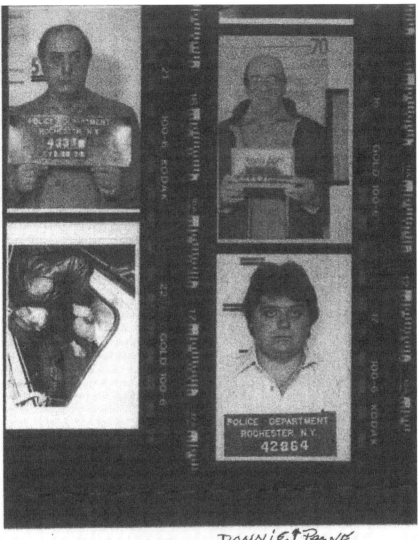

Rochester Police Department mugshots, page three. Top left is Sam Amico. Top right is Rochester Mafia Captain Joe "The Hop" Rossi. Bottom right is Rochester Mafia Soldier Donnie Paone.

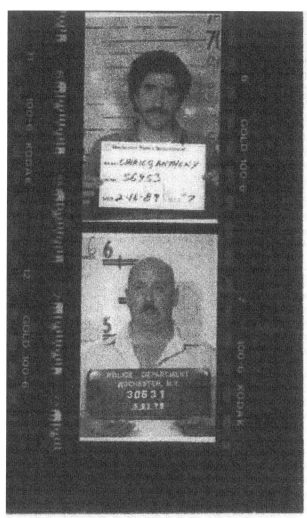

Rochester Police Department mugshots, page four. Top photo is Rochester Mafia B-Team member Anthony Chirico and bottom photo is C-Team leader Thomas "The Eagle" Taylor.

Part 2
The Aftermath

Chapter 1
The Fiorino Murder

**Thomas Taylor
aka
"The Eagle"**

The formation of the "C-Team" was a direct result of pressure put on certain individuals by "made" members of the Rochester Mafia, namely the A-team. Several individuals had been threatened with death including Thomas Torpey, Thomas Taylor, and Thomas Pelusio. Taylor and Torpey were both former members of the A Team. They were both in "Sammy G's" car when it exploded. But there had been a falling out.

Torpey's drug habit kept getting worse. He refused to pay the "vig" on his gambling joint. Threats were made on his life by the Rochester Mafia. Taylor also had a contract out on him by the same people for different reasons. The last straw was when Fiorino slapped Thomas Torpey when he (Fiorino) came to collect the "vig" on Torpey's joint, but was rebuffed by him.

A frustrated Fiorino told Torpey, "You can bleed like anyone else."

Fearing that they would both be killed by the Rochester Mafia, Taylor and Torpey went on the offensive and struck first. They hired an out of town hit-man that Taylor had met while he was incarcerated in Attica State Prison named Joseph Sullivan.

Sullivan was hired to kill both the "Underboss," Dick Marino, and John Fiorino, "Captain," in the Rochester Mafia. After several meetings at a Greece hotel, a loose-knit plan was hatched and put into operation.

Several days were spent attempting to locate the targets before someone was able to contact Fiorino and set up a meeting. A man called "The Eagle" had called Fiorino's home on the night of his death and asked to speak with John. John left his home to go meet "The Eagle" and he never returned. The Eagle was Thomas Taylor's nickname.

Planning A Murder

Louis DiGiulio

Louis DiGiulio was the getaway driver for Joe Sullivan on the night Sullivan murdered John Fiorino. DiGuilio was originally charged with murder and was about to stand trial for that charge, but the night before the trial began, DiGuilio turned states-evidence and agreed to testify against his co-defendants in exchange for a reduced sentence.

His testimony, if believed, provided a timeline of events and gave a clear picture of the planning and execution of John Fiorino's murder.

Louis DiGiulio testified that on **Dec. 14, 1981**, he was on his way to Thomas Taylor's apartment in the Green Leaf Meadows complex in Greece when he stopped at a gasoline station at the corner of Lake Avenue and Stutson Street to buy gas and cigarettes. By chance, Taylor and Torpey drove into the station in Taylor's brown 1979 Thunderbird.

"Hey, Louie," they said. **"How ya doing? Sully's in town."**

DiGiulio testified he'd first met the small, muscular Sullivan a year before at Taylor's house. He next saw him during the summer of 1981 at a cookout Taylor held near Hamlin Beach.

On **Dec. 15, 1981**, DiGiulio met Torpey and Taylor at Taylor's apartment. DiGiulio said they told him to go to the Marriott Inn on West Ridge Road in Greece to meet Sullivan who would be staying on the seventh floor under a fake name. Torpey and Taylor were to show up later. DiGiulio testified that he arrived at Sullivan's room at 6:45p.m. When the hit man answered the door, he was holding a large hunting knife inside a sheaf. On the bed was a pump-action sawed-off shotgun, an automatic handgun and a silencer.

Sullivan asked DiGiulio, **"What do you got for me?"**

DiGiulio replied, **"There's two guys, one's an 'Underboss,' one's a 'Captain."**

John Fiorino had been identified by law enforcement officials as a "Captain" in Rochester's organized Crime Family. After half an hour's conversation, they came up with a sketchy plan. DiGiulio and Sullivan would drive around to various bars, hoping to run across Fiorino and Richard Marino. "I'd point them out to Joe and he was going to blast them," DiGiulio testified. Torpey and Taylor were to follow in Taylor's car, which they'd use as a "crash car" if they saw DiGiulio and Sullivan were being chased by a police car; Torpey and Taylor were to crash into it.

Later, when Sullivan was on trial, defense lawyers ridiculed DiGiulio's story, pointing out Torpey was hiding out from police in December of 1981. Why would Taylor and Torpey risk crashing into a police car in Taylor's car in the area of a gangland murder, they asked. But DiGiulio didn't waver in his testimony. He said that on the night of **Dec. 15, 1981** the four drove in two cars to search for Fiorino and Marino. Sullivan was driving his 1977 peach-colored Cadillac and Taylor was driving his Thunderbird.

They had drinks at Jason's restaurant on Hudson Avenue, the former Blue Gardenia Restaurant in the Empire Plaza and a bar on East Ridge Road, all in Irondequoit. But they couldn't find either of the men they were planning to kill.

They decided to drive to Tommy's restaurant on East Avenue. On the way they spotted a familiar truck parked in front of a gambling club on St. Paul Street. It belonged to Joseph "Joe the Hop" Rossi, Fiorino's Mob associate and close friend. DiGiulio testified he went inside and told Rossi that Taylor was at Tommy's and wanted to talk to him. At the bar, Taylor said to Rossi,

"Why don't you give John (Fiorino) a call? Tell him to come out and have a couple of drinks."

Sullivan and Torpey waited outside in the car. Rossi made the call, but Fiorino never showed.

On **Dec. 17, 1981**, DiGiulio picked Sullivan up at the Marriott and helped him carry his suitcases down to the Cadillac after he checked out. The two met Torpey and Taylor at Trebor's Restaurant on State Street, where DiGiulio said they ate lunch, drank wine and cocktails, and snorted cocaine. The group left Trebor's at about 3:30 p.m. and planned to meet again two hours later at Jason's, where they would try to lure Fiorino to kill him.

On the night of the murder, Taylor said he was having trouble getting Fiorino to Jason's, but Fiorino said he would be at the Blue Gardenia about 7 p.m. By 5:30, DiGiulio and Sullivan were waiting in the parking lot at the Blue Gardenia. Torpey and Taylor arrived-shortly afterward. A short time later, John Fiorino arrived. Fiorino pulled up in a green Lincoln Continental and started walking toward the entrance of the restaurant. It was about 6:45.

"That him," Sullivan asked DiGiulio.

"I can't be sure," answered DiGiulio.

"Is it him or isn't it," persisted Sullivan.

"Yeah, it's him," DiGiulio replied while nodding his head. Then Sullivan, concealing a sawed-off shotgun underneath his coat, stepped out of the car and walked toward Fiorino.

"I heard the shots," DiGiulio testified. "I looked. I saw John drop, Sullivan started walking back toward the Cadillac. He hesitated for a moment, turned and walked back toward Fiorino's body. He stood over the body and deliberately fired another blast into Fiorino's head."

Sullivan told DiGiulio to keep the car's lights turned off, drive slowly out of the plaza and stay calm.

Fiorino Shot Dead at Blue Gardenia

Dec. 18. 1981 Democrat & Chronicle

John "Johnny Flowers" Fiorino, was Vice-President of Teamsters Local #398 in Rochester, N.Y. He was murdered on **Dec. 17, 1981** outside of the Blue Gardenia Restaurant in Irondequoit, N.Y. by Joseph "Mad Dog" Sullivan, and on the orders of "C Team" Mafia leaders Thomas Torpey and Thomas Taylor.

The driver, Louis DiGuilio, was caught at the scene and taken into custody. The shooter, Joseph Sullivan, escaped on foot after firing upon officer DiGiovanni of the Irondequoit Police Department. (1)

Mob figure slain in Irondequoit

At the time of his death, The FBI considered John Fiorino to have been a "made" member and "Captain" of the Rochester Mafia Crime Family. John Fiorino had also allegedly become an informant and was cooperating with the U.S. Organized Crime Strike Force, sources said.

Other sources claimed Fiorino began cooperating with authorities around April of 1981, fearing that he would be indicted for the murder of B-Team leader Thomas DiDio. Fiorino allegedly gave police the names of the three suspected killers. (2)

Victim Was Informant

John Fiorino
Vice-President
of Teamsters
Local #398.

Teamsters Local #398 in Rochester, N.Y. had long been controlled by the Rochester Mafia. As far back as 1959, federal authorities began investigations and held inquiries attempting to discover the ties between organized labor and organized crime in Rochester.

In the 1970's, Senate hearings identified Teamsters Local #398 as being controlled by Sammy Gingello and organized crime. Gingello and Fiorino held leadership positions in both the Mafia and the union. They were also partners in a trucking business. They used their positions to "put the squeeze" on independent truckers by putting so many demands on them that they were forced out of business. Then Sam-Jon Trucking (**Sam** Gingello and **John** Fiorino) would get all the jobs.

Fiorino and Gingello were together on March 2, 1978 when a pipe bomb exploded outside of the Blue Gardenia Restaurant but failed to kill its intended target, Sammy Gingello. Gingello was killed just eight weeks later.

In January of 1980, Fiorino was subpoenaed to U.S. District Court during the racketeering and weapons trials of the "B Team" members of the Rochester Mafia. He testified about the attempted assassination of Gingello in March of 1978. Sources claimed that Fiorino was cooperating with the Organized Crime Strike Force at the time of his death, but it could not be determined if Fiorino actually testified before he was murdered. (3)

Resurgence of Mob War Feared

Dec. 19, 1981 Democrat and Chronicle

    Authorities feared that the murder of John Fiorino would be the spark that reignited the "Rochester Mob Wars." Thomas Torpey had cut ties with the Mafia leaders about four months prior in August of 1981, when he started refusing to pay the "vig" on his gambling joint.

    Immediately after Fiorino's murder, authorities executed a search warrant on Torpey's gambling parlor, located at 251 Lyell Ave. in Rochester. A member of the club, Charles Perotti lll, was at the club when it was raided. Police made no arrests that night and left after about an hour. Perotti said, at the time, police had been across the street doing surveillance on the club ever since the shooting.

    At the very least authorities believed Fiorino's murder was a clear message, a warning, to A-Team leaders to step down. Torpey and Taylor were making moves to take over control of Rochester's organized crime activities. Resurgence of the Mob War was sure to follow. (4)

Young Men's Social Club Destroyed by Fire

Only weeks later, the Young Men's Social Club, a long established gambling parlor in the city, located at 251 Lyell Ave., was destroyed by fire on **Feb. 5, 1982**. The club was owned and operated by Thomas Torpey, a leading member of the C-Team.

Reputed underworld figure Thomas Torpey talks with a fireman at the scene of a mysterious fire that destroyed Torpey's gambling parlor at 251 Lyell Ave. on Feb. 5, 1982.

The cause of the fire was "undetermined." Despite rumors of possible "retaliation," authorities were leaning toward accidental causes rather than arson. They had originally labeled the fire suspicious, but later changed that determination. (74)

Money Found in the Walls at 253 Lyell Avenue

"The firemen upon breaking through the walls of the upstairs apartment found stacks of money hidden in the walls. None of the money belonged to us."

Back in the 1940s and 1950s, the building that housed Torpey's gambling joint at 253 Lyell Ave. was rented by Billy Terra and his brother, Joe. The Terra brothers operated a store called the Rochester Amusement Company.

> The Terras were accused of illegal possession of the sub-machinegun, found in a pinball machine in a raid by Rochester and State Police on the store at 253 Lyell Ave., on July 19, 1949. Joe Terra operated the store under the name of Rochester Amusement Company.

June 7, 1950 Democrat and Chronicle

State police raided the store at 253 Lyell Ave. on July 19, 1949. Police found more than amusement machines. Hidden inside of a pinball machine police discovered a sub-machine gun. The brothers were arrested on weapons charges. Police also found two pistols, stolen money orders, and counterfeit money.

Both brothers were eventually sentenced to prison. Apparently police never found all of the money hidden in the walls of the building and the money remained there undetected until the 1982 fire, more than 30 years later. (72)

253 Lyell Avenue

Chapter 2
Mad Dog Sullivan

Mad Dog Killer Who Fled Attica in 1971 is Caught

Eighteen days after Torpey's gambling joint burned to the ground, Joseph "Mad Dog" Sullivan, a suspect in more than seven murders, three assaults and numerous bank robberies, was finally apprehended by the FBI on **Feb. 23, 1982,** at the Denonville Inn in Penfield, N.Y.

Following an anonymous tip, ten FBI Agents surrounded the hotel where Sullivan was reportedly staying with his longtime girlfriend, Jamie Palmieri. When Sullivan and Palmieri emerged from the hotel, Sullivan was wearing a bullet proof vest and he

Mad Dog" Sullivan was arrested at The Denonville Inn (above) in Penfield, N.Y.,

was armed with a .38 caliber revolver and an M-16 automatic rifle.

FBI agents quickly moved in and surrounded the couple. Clinton Van Zant, the acting agent in charge of Rochester's FBI office said, "When the agents confronted 'Mad Dog' Sullivan, he just smiled and gave up without incident."

Sullivan had once escaped from Attica Prison in 1971. He reportedly stayed in shape by doing 1,000 pushups and running ten miles every day. (5)

Prosecutor Wants to See Mad Dog

The picture on the right shows Joseph Sullivan on the day he was arrested for the murder of Teamster Vice-President John Fiorino. At the time of his arraignment, Sullivan was described by police as a pivotal figure in the murder of two women and a six-year old boy, and a suspect in 11 other murders.

Joseph "Mad Dog" Sullivan was captured at the Denonville Inn in Penfield, N.Y. on Feb. 23, 1982.

Joseph Sullivan and Brian Molese were prime suspects in the murder of Molese's estranged wife Alice, her friend, and roommate Marcia Ferrell and Ferrell's six-year old son, Harry. The trio had been found with their throats slashed and multiple stab wounds.

Sullivan had met Molese at the old Manhattan House of Detention. Molese was serving time for arson and Sullivan for the 1965 murder of a man in a barroom. At some point, police sources said, Sullivan and Molese had a falling out. There was some sort of dispute over money, which led to Sullivan attempting to murder both Molese and Molese's roommate Chris Crosthwaite in a Greenwich Village apartment.

On June 8, 1981, Sullivan shot them both in the face and head with a small caliber weapon that had a homemade silencer attached to it. Both men's lives were spared, primarily due to the silencer diminishing the velocity of the bullets. New York City Police immediately put out an arrest warrant for Sullivan at the time, but he remained a fugitive until his February 1982 capture in Penfield, N.Y. Sullivan was arraigned on attempted homicide charges in connection to that incident. (6)

The falling out between Molese and Sullivan was over the insurance money that Molese allegedly received after his (Molese) wife's death. Sullivan was supposed to receive a percentage of the insurance policy for his part of the murder of Molese's wife.

Gail Sullivan convinced Joe that Molese had already collected on the insurance policy and was holding out on paying Joe his share. Joe Sullivan told Thomas Taylor that his wife Gail was with him when he shot Molese and the other man.

That's probably what the law used as leverage to get Gail Sullivan to testify against Torpey and Taylor at their murder trial. Why else would she testify against her husband's co-conspirators?

The threat of taking her children away from her and possible jail time for her involvement in the Molese shooting seemed to be enough for Gail to testify, for the police, about events that occurred at the cottage on the lake, and prior to the Fiorino murder.

Thomas Taylor had rented a cottage on Lake Ontario for two weeks. One week for family and one week for friends. During the week for friends the guest list included the Pelusio brothers, Joe Sullivan, his wife Gail, and Louis DiGiulio.

But Gail Sullivan put Torpey at the cottage when he wasn't even there. This testimony was necessary to further the prosecutions theory that the conspiracy to kill John Fiorino began at the cottage. That was what Louis DiGiulio was testifying to after he flipped. Since DiGiulio was a participant in the crime the prosecution needed a collaborating witness, which was Gail Sullivan.

Sullivan Arraigned on Robbery Charges

On **Feb. 25, 1982**, Joseph "Mad Dog" Sullivan was arraigned in Monroe County Court on murder charges for the Dec. 17, 1981 shot-gun slaying of John Fiorino. The next day he was transported to the U.S. District Court in Syracuse, N.Y. where he was arraigned on federal bank robbery charges for a bank robbery he committed on Dec. 13, 1981, in Utica, N.Y.

Federal law stated that Sullivan must be tried on the bank robbery charges within 90 days. Following the completion of that trial, Sullivan was brought back to Monroe County to face the murder charge. (7)

Joseph Sullivan exits a car on Clinton Street in Syracuse, N.Y., arriving at the federal courthouse for his arraignment on bank robbery charges on Feb. 26, 1982. (70)

Thomas Taylor and Pelusio Brothers Assault Moe Alaimo at the 44 Club

On Friday night, **March 12, 1982**, Thomas Taylor, Thomas Torpey and two of the Pelusio brothers, Michael and Thomas, assaulted Samuel "Moe" Alaimo, at the Caserta Political and Social Club, "44 Club," located at 44 Lake Ave. Police were following the suspects that evening, having done periodic surveillance on Taylor ever since the Fiorino murder. But the police did not witness what happened inside the club.

Alaimo was allegedly beaten in the face, head and back with a broom handle and then kicked in the chest and throat. Charlie Russo was also present in the Club that evening. He too received a beating. Officials said that they discovered a motive for the crime but they refused to disclose it.

The three men were all arraigned on the following day, **March 13, 1982**. (55)

Grand jury to hear of assault

3 reputed mob figures charged in beating

By Jim Redmond
Democrat and Chronicle

The assault case against three reputed organized crime figures accused of beating a man inside a Lake Avenue gambling parlor Friday night is expected to be presented to a grand jury tomorrow.

Thomas E. Taylor, 41, Thomas A. Pelusio, 35, and Michael Pelusio, 27, were arraigned in City Court yesterday on second-degree assault charges in the beating, felony offenses.

Samuel Alaimo, 34, of 59 Fifth St., was beaten minutes after the three men and two others who weren't charged went into the Caserta Political and Social Club, 44 Lake Ave., shortly before 7 p.m., Rochester police said.

Alaimo was beaten on the face, head and back with a broom handle and then kicked in the chest and throat. He was treated at Genesee Hospital.

Taylor and the Pelusios were under police surveillance when they went into the club, but police outside didn't see the attack, said police Capt. Thomas Conroy. Local organized crime figures have been under surveillance periodically since the Dec. 17 shotgun slaying of reputed mobster John Fiorino.

Police identified the club, commonly known as the "44 Club," as a known gambling parlor controlled by mob figures and have identified Alaimo as an associate of area organized crime figures. Officials have a found a motive behind the attack but refused to disclose it.

"It's going into the facts of the case," said Assistant Monroe County District Attorney Melchor Castro. "It's going beyond what I'm permitted to tell you."

Thomas Pelusio, of 96 Laureiton Road, and Michael Pelusio, of 418 Lake Ave., were freed yesterday after posting the $1,000 bail each.

Monroe County Court Judge Andrew Celli set bail for Taylor at $10,000, which was posted after arraignment.

City Court judges weren't permitted to set bail for Taylor because he has been convicted of two previous felonies, Castro said. In 1961, Taylor was convicted of second-degree assault for attacking a Greece police officer. In 1964, he was convicted of attempted extortion, for which he served eight years in prison.

March 14, 1982 Democrat and Chronicle

Children Find Shotgun Believed Used in Slaying

March 16, 1982 Democrat and Chronicle

On **March 14, 1982,** children playing in the backyard of an Irondequoit home discovered a strange object protruding from the melting snow. A rusty sawed-off shot gun. The weapon did not belong to the homeowners, who promptly reported the find to local police.

Richard Baug's home, at 212 Queensboro Road in Irondequoit, where the gun was found, is only two blocks away from where the murder of John Fiorino took place three months previously, on Dec. 17, 1981. Police suspected that the recovered gun was the murder weapon in the Fiorino case.

On the night of the murder the suspected shooter escaped from police after firing four shot gun blasts at officer Michael DiGiovanni, who pursued the suspect on foot after the suspect abandoned the crashed getaway car. The suspect apparently ran through some yards and ditched the gun two blocks away, where it was eventually discovered.

Police had searched the area immediately after the shooting, but several days of freshly fallen snow impeded their efforts to find the discarded weapon. Three months after the shooting police finally had both the suspected murderer and murder weapon in custody. (8)

Later that evening...

Police Confiscate Thomas Taylor's Car, No Charges Filed

Police confiscate mob figure's car

Reputed organized crime figure, Thomas E. Taylor, who was arraigned Saturday on assault charges and released on $10,000 bail, led police on a chase last night along Lake Avenue to his house in Greece, police said.

March 15, 1982
Democrat and Chronicle

Sunday night, **March 14, 1982**, police were once again following reputed organized crime figure Thomas Taylor. The officer following Taylor claimed that he witnessed Taylor driving through red lights on Lake Avenue. He also claimed that Taylor was speeding, although he never pulled Taylor over.

Instead, police followed Taylor to his home on Greenleaf Road in Greece and Taylor went inside. He allegedly would not allow the police to enter without a search warrant. According to Capt. Thomas Conroy, Taylor's car was then towed by police as "possible evidence of a crime," despite the fact that Taylor was never charged with any crime. Capt. Conroy further explained, that, "It's the departments policy to tow a vehicle that's believed to be involved in a crime, if the suspect has fled."

The broomstick assault case was presented to the grand Jury on Monday, **March 15, 1982**. Assistant Monroe County District Attorney Mel Castro said, as of **March 16, 1982,** two days after the traffic incident, that no charges had been filed against Taylor. But police said that they were still "considering" filing charges against him. Then finally, three days later, on **March 17, 1982**, City Court Judge Alphonse Cassetti issued an arrest warrant for Taylor for the traffic infractions, and Rochester and Gates police arrested Taylor at 8 p.m. as he left Little Anthony's Restaurant at 2389 Lyell Ave. in Gates. He was then released after posting $450 bail and he was arraigned the following morning, on **March 18, 1982**. (56)

Pictured at left is Bobby Comfort. Comfort was notorious for the 1972 Hotel Pierre robbery, in New York City. In 1982, Comfort was an active C-Team member. When police chased Thomas Taylor down Lake Avenue and confronted him about his driving infractions, Taylor just laughed and said, "I wasn't driving, Bobby Comfort was." Then they all went into Taylor's house and refused to come out.

According to Thomas Taylor, Bobby Comfort and Thomas Torpey were in the car with him. Taylor explained, "It was St. Patrick's Day. We weren't stopping at any red lights on Lake Avenue because we were joking about the red lights being 'Orangemen.' The Orangemen are a radical group of Irish Protestants, dressed in bright orange vests, who parade through Irish Catholic neighborhoods each year, terrorizing the residents. Therefore, we were not stopping."

He continued, "The cops didn't stop us because they could not catch us. And they can't enter your home unless you have committed a felony. It was only traffic charges by some Irish guys on St. Patrick's Day that might have had too much to drink."

But Tom Taylor's daughter, Laura, remembers the event vividly and tells the story much more dramatically. "I was in my early 20's, I had just found Jesus! I was at my mom's house near where my dad lived. I was watching the news. There was a live report about the police chasing some Mobsters.

"They chased them to a home in Greece right down the street from me and they had the place surrounded. All of a sudden I realized the breaking news was about my father! The house on T.V., which was surrounded by the Feds, was his Greenleaf townhouse. He had barricaded himself, Tom Torpey and two others inside.

"I said to my mom, I'm going down there and share the Gospel with them! When I arrived the Feds were everywhere and had everything cornered off. One was talking on a bullhorn telling my dad to come out! I pressed my head against the steering wheel and prayed. God, if this is your will you'll make me invisible so I can get to my dad. I took a deep breath and off I went.

"I got out off my car and walked right past the barricade where the Feds had the house cornered off, right up the sidewalk, past another fed in the bushes, and right to my dad's front door! I knocked and said dad, it's me, Laura!"

Before he opened the door he asked me, "Did someone send you?"

I said, "No." He then asked me, "Is anyone near you?"

I said, "Yes, there's a guy hiding in the bushes near me." My Dad asked, "Do you think you can make it in if I opened and shut the door quickly?"

I said, "Yes." He opened the door and pulled me in quickly and shut the door!

He was very surprised I walked right past the feds at the barricade and another fed in the bush near the front door, and into the townhouse!

I said, "It was *Divine Intervention*, dad!"

Taylor and Marino Indicted

Taylor and Marino indicted

A Monroe County grand jury indicted reputed Mafia figures Thomas Taylor and Richard Marino in separate cases Thursday. Both men are free on bail.

Taylor, 42, of Greenleaf Meadow Road, Greece, was indicted along with two others on second-degree assault charges in connection with the beating of a Fifth Street man in a Lake Avenue gambling parlor March 12.

Marino, 42, of 68 Venice Circle, Irondequoit, faces menacing and third-degree criminal possession of a weapon charges. He is accused of threatening a man with a gun.

Indicted along with Taylor in the beating of 34-year-old Samuel Alaimo were brothers Thomas A. Pelusio, 45, of 96 Laurelton Road and Michael A. Pelusio, 27, of 418 Lake Ave. The three are charged with beating Alaimo with a broom handle inside the Caserta Social and Political Club, 44 Lake Ave., better known as the Club 44. Alaimo was treated at Genesee Hospital after the attack.

Marino is accused of placing a .22-caliber pistol to the forehead of John Lopez on Dec. 15 at the Bay & Goodman Grill, 906 N. Goodman St.

Thomas Taylor and Richard Marino were both indicted on **March 18, 1982**, but for separate cases. Taylor was indicted with two other men for second degree assault in connection with a broomstick beating inflicted on Samuel Alaimo at the 44 Club, a known gambling parlor on State Street.

Richard Marino, Rochester Mafia "Underboss," was indicted for menacing and criminal possession of a weapon for threatening a man with a gun. Marino allegedly placed a .22 caliber pistol to the forehead of a man named John Lopez at the Bay and Goodman Grill at 906 N. Goodman St. on Dec. 15, 1981. (53)

The murder trial of reputed mobsters Thomas E. Taylor and Thomas M. Torpey, who are charged in the shotgun slaying of John N. Fiorino Dec. 17, 1981, will take place after Taylor's trial on assault charges.

Taylor was indicted March 18, 1982, on assault charges in connection with an incident at the Caserta Political and Social Club, 44 Lake Ave. He is accused with brothers Thomas A. and Michael A. Pelusio of injuring Samuel Alaimo with a broomstick.

Social Club With Links to Mob Hit by Fire of Unknown Cause

Firefighters take a breather and a television cameraman records the scene yesterday morning after a fire was extinguished at a social club that's linked to mobsters. The fire started near an inside wall. Investigators are trying to determine the cause.

Fire damages social club linked to mob

The Yamaha Social Club, located at 221 Franklin St., was heavily damaged by fire on **March 22, 1982**. The club was associated with organized crime and tied to Rochester's established Mafia leaders (A-Team).

There had been several gambling arrests made at the club in the past, and the month before, "Moe" Alaimo, a reputed underworld figure, had $30,000 in cash on him when he was stopped by police outside of the club.

Anthony Alongi, the club's operator, told police he left the building at 8 a.m. that morning and hadn't noticed anything askew. The origin of the fire was unknown. (57)

Mad Dog Denies Suffolk County Slayings

On **March 25, 1982**, Sullivan was brought to Riverhead where he was arraigned on two charges of attempted murder. He was arraigned in Suffolk County on an eight count indictment charging murder, attempted murder, robbery and assault. He pleaded innocent to the charges.

Sullivan was a suspect in 11 murders and a dozen bank robberies at the time. (9)

'Mad Dog' Sullivan denies 2 slaying charges in Suffolk County

United Press International

RIVERHEAD — Joseph John "Mad Dog" Sullivan, a suspect in 11 killings, pleaded innocent yesterday to two slayings.

Sullivan, 42, an ex-convict and escape artist, was surrounded by a dozen U.S. marshals and county police officers as he was brought into Suffolk County Court in handcuffs.

Sullivan was brought to Riverhead from Manhattan, where he was arraigned earlier yesterday on two charges of attempted murder.

He was arraigned in Suffolk on an eight-count indictment charging murder, attempted murder, robbery and assault.

Sullivan was arrested last month by the FBI in upstate Penfield, a Rochester suburb.

Police said he is a suspect in 11 killings in Suffolk County, upstate New York, Manhattan and New Jersey and has been linked to a dozen bank robberies throughout the state.

March 26, 1982 Democrat and Chronicle

Nicholas Mastrodonato is Murdered

Man linked to local mob shot to death in coin store

Nicholas Mastrodonato slain, but motive remains a mystery

By Gary Gerew
Democrat and Chronicle

Several police agencies, including the FBI, are investigating the slaying yesterday afternoon of Nicholas Mastrodonato, who police identified as an organized crime figure.

Mastrodonato, 33, died at Park Ridge Hospital about 30 minutes after he was shot several times about 3 p.m. as he worked at a gold- and silver-buying store in Gates.

Gates Police Chief Thomas Roche said robbery hasn't been eliminated as a motive, but he said Mastrodonato's killer apparently began firing as he entered the store, Mr. Gold's Coin Shop at 481 Spencerport Road.

Police put together this description of Mastrodonato's killer: A stocky man between 20 and 35 who wore sunglasses, a blue jacket, blue pants and a blue baseball cap. The man had bushy, sandy-colored hair that stuck out around the sides and back of the baseball cap.

Roche said ballistics tests won't be completed until today, but it's believed Mastrodonato was shot with a .45-caliber pistol, based on shell casings found in the store.

"It appears the person went there specifically to shoot a firearm," Roche said. Roche said investigators are still trying to complete an inventory of the store, but he said there was money, including $20 bills, left in the cash register.

"The cabinets in the store weren't cleaned out either," Roche said. "If the motive was robbery, it appears the shooting happened before anything was taken."

An autopsy will be performed today. Roche said Mastrodonato was apparently shot at least once in the head, but there may have been as many as nine shots fired.

Roche said there had been no reports of robberies at stores near the coin shop in the past year.

Because of Mastrodonato's association with organized crime figures, police are also considering that may be a motive for his death. Mastrodonato, police sources said, was linked to an insurgent group within local organized crime lead by Thomas Torpey and Thomas Taylor.

"He (Mastrodonato) was involved with them, but he wasn't a sworn member of the Mafia," said one law enforcement official. "He was on the fringe."

Some law enforcement officials believe the insurgent group was involved in last December's slaying of John Fiorino in Irondequoit.

Capt. Thomas Conroy, head of the Rochester Police Department's special criminal investigation unit, said he and several officers from his unit were assisting the Gates police investigation, as were investigators from the Monroe County Sheriff's Department and other organized crime investigators from other police departments.

Roche said there isn't any evidence that yesterday's killing was related to organized

TURN TO PAGE 3A

May 26, 1982 Democrat and Chronicle

Several police agencies, including the FBI, were involved in investigating the **May 25, 1982** shooting death of Nicholas Mastrodonato. He was shot several times and died while working at his coin shop in Gates.

Robbery had not been ruled out as a motive, although police say that the killer entered the store firing shots at the victim, and nothing appeared to be missing. Mastrodonato had ties to an insurgent Mafia faction labeled the "C Team," led by Thomas Torpey and Thomas Taylor, that police believed were responsible for the murder of John Fiorino. (10)

Tommy Taylor said, "Nicky was a good man. He and Bobby Comfort were business partners in the Mister Gold store that Nicky was killed in. I used to tease Bobby because he had masterminded the 'Pierre Hotel Robbery' on New Year's Eve that netted millions. I would kid him that now he was buying gold instead of stealing it."

"Joe Sullivan called Bobby Comfort after the Blue Gardenia shooting and he and Nicky drove over and picked him up. They took Sullivan to Nicky's house and then got him out of town. When Torpey and I were in jail, Bobby Comfort was running the C-Team and forwarding orders to others."

Chapter 3
DiGuilio Turns Informant

Louis DiGiulio was arrested for the murder of John Fiorino. He was jailed and remained silent for several months until the evening before his trial. DiGiulio decided to turn "state's evidence" and testify against his co-conspirators in exchange for a lighter sentence. He then entered into the Federal Witness Protection Program.

Testimony to Start in DiGuilio Murder Trial

Testimony to start in DiGuilio trial

Testimony is expected to begin today in the murder trial of Louis DiGuilio, who is accused of driving the get-away car used by the gunman who killed reputed organized crime figure John Fiorino outside the Blue Gardenia Restaurant last December.

DiGuilio, 25, of 52 Sunset St., is charged with second-degree murder and attempted murder in connection with the slaying. He's accused of driving the car for reputed hit man Joseph John Sullivan on Dec. 17 when Sullivan allegedly killed Fiorino with a shotgun.

DiGuilio also is charged with attempted murder in connection with shots Sullivan is accused of firing at Irondequoit police officer Michael DiGiovanni as he chased the car after Fiorino's shooting.

Sullivan, whose federal trial in Syracuse on bank robbery charges was scheduled to begin yesterday, will be tried on murder charges here separately.

**June 8, 1982
Democrat and Chronicle**

Testimony in the trial of Louis DiGuilio for the murder of John Fiorino was scheduled to begin on **June 8, 1982**. DiGuilio was the accused getaway driver for Joseph Sullivan after the shotgun slaying of John Fiorino on Dec. 17, 1981 at the Blue Gardenia Restaurant in Irondequoit, N.Y.

DiGuilio was also charged with attempted murder in connection to the shots that Sullivan fired at Irondequoit police officer Michael DiGiovanni during the attempted getaway.

Joseph Sullivan was in Syracuse, N.Y. at the time, standing trial for bank robbery. His trial had started the previous day on June 7, 1982. His murder trial in Rochester was scheduled for a later date. (11)

But Louis DiGuilio never did go on trial that day. Instead, DiGuilio broke his silence and gave up his co-conspirators, proving once again that the Mafia's so called code of "omerta" is just plain bullshit!

DiGiulio Ends His Silence
Torpey and Taylor Arrested
for the Murder of John Fiorino

June 9, 1982 Democrat and Chronicle

On **June 8, 1982,** Thomas Torpey and Thomas Taylor were arrested for ordering the murder of John Fiorino. The arrest was the direct result of Louis DiGiulio, a participant in the Fiorino murder, ratting out his co-conspirators. After spending more than five months in jail, refusing to talk, DiGiulio broke his silence after Torpey and Taylor allegedly refused to "take care of" him while he was in jail.

DiGiulio said he could not even get Torpey or Taylor to send him $50 for spending money while he was incarcerated. That was DiGuilio's stated reason for becoming an informant.

That was an absolute lie, according to Thomas Taylor. "Louie's bail was $100,000," said Taylor. "I personally gave Louie's father $1,000 in cash and I gave Tom Pelusio $5,000 to retain Les Bradshaw whose fee was $15,000. I also gave him two ounces of coke to sell toward the remainder. Cocaine was going for roughly $2,300 to $2,700 an ounce at the time, depending on who you sold it to." Les Bradshaw remained as DiGiulio's lawyer right up until DiGiulio entered into the Federal Witness Protection Program.

> "I was left hanging... I was there to drive the car. I didn't think I was actually killing anybody. I knew I was involved in a conspiracy.... I want to turn state's evidence."

Those were the words of Louis DiGiulio, Mob associate turned informant.

For more than five months while awaiting trial, DiGiulio refused to cooperate with authorities. But on **June 6, 1982**, on the eve of his second-degree murder trial, DiGiulio broke his silence and turned police informant, implicating Thomas Torpey and Thomas Taylor in the Fiorino murder. Torpey and Taylor were arrested a few days later after DiGiulio agreed to testify against them and Sullivan.

Taylor said, **"I couldn't even say how I took care of that rat bastard, because I was now facing trial."**

DiGiulio's deal also required testimony against Torpey and Taylor. DiGiulio gave four days of testimony in Monroe County Court, testimony the defense called "the gospel according to Louie." Felix V. Lapine, Torpey's lawyer, and John F. Speranza, who represented Taylor, labeled DiGiulio a conniving liar, saying he made up the story for the lighter sentence.

As Torpey and Taylor watched intently, sometimes taking notes, Lapine and Speranza grilled DiGiulio, who sat impassive behind dark-tinted glasses. In his testimony, DiGiulio spoke of growing tension and animosity between rival organized crime factions in 1981. On one side was Thomas Taylor and his friend Thomas Torpey, who ran a lucrative gambling club on Lyell Avenue known as Torpey's joint. On the other were the long-established members of the Rochester underworld, including John Fiorino.

The street-tough DiGiulio, a convicted burglar and thief, said he met Torpey about 12 years prior in the 44 Club, a gambling parlor on Lake Avenue. DiGiulio also provided key testimony in the murder trial of Joseph Sullivan, who was convicted in 1982 of firing the shotgun blast that killed John Fiorino on Dec. 17, 1981.

Without question, DiGiulio had benefited by testifying for the prosecution. He and Sullivan were initially charged with second-degree murder in the Fiorino killing. DiGiulio was supposed to be tried first. But on the eve of his trial, he agreed to cooperate with the District Attorney's office. Later, his testimony was crucial in obtaining Sullivan's murder conviction in September of that year.

In exchange for his cooperation, DiGiulio was allowed to plead guilty to a lesser charge of conspiracy to commit murder. For that crime, prosecutors recommended a five to ten year sentence in a federal prison, rather than a state facility. He had been looking at a maximum sentence of life in prison for a second-degree murder conviction. He was also later placed into the Witness Protection Program. (12)

Chapter 4
$500,000 Bail for Taylor

Thomas Taylor has 4 Convictions for Assault, Served 8 Years for Extortion

Thomas Taylor first made headlines in 1960 when he pled guilty to an assault charge and then failed to show up for sentencing, twice. The headlines read, 'Warrant Ordered in Assault Case.' Taylor was eventually sentenced to three months probation.

June 9, 1982 Democrat and Chronicle

Following his first conviction, Taylor quickly racked up three more assault convictions, including two on police officers. While awaiting sentencing on a 1964 extortion charge, Taylor allegedly assaulted two jail guards. He was later convicted of that charge.

Earlier that year, 1982, Taylor was charged again with assault in regard to the 44 Club incident. Taylor and two other men entered the 44 Club located at 44 Lake Ave. The club was a gambling joint run my Samuel "Moe" Alaimo. Alaimo, allegedly, was assaulted with a broomstick and had dimes shoved in his mouth by Thomas Taylor.

According to Taylor, Alaimo threatened to call "Blue Eyes," who was Rochester Mob Captain Thomas Marotta. Taylor said, "I put the dimes in his mouth in case he needed them to make the call."

"Alaimo called 'Blue Eyes,' (Thomas Marotta). Marotta called Sgt. Grande and Sgt. Grande picked us up at the bar where the Mob was supposed to come get us." (13)

$500,000 bail for Taylor

On **June 15, 1982**, a bail hearing was held for Thomas Taylor, who stood accused of murder for hiring Joseph Sullivan to kill John Fiorino.

Earlier that month Judge Bergin had set bail for Thomas Torpey, Taylor's co-conspirator and co-defendant, at $500,000. Assistant Monroe County District Attorney Donald J. Wisner was seeking the same bail for Taylor.

Defense Attorney for Thomas Taylor, John Speranza, sparred with Assistant Monroe County District Attorney Donald J. Wisner in court over the amount of bail placed on Taylor. Wisner was seeking bail in the amount of $500,000 for Taylor due to his extensive criminal history. Speranza claimed that $100,000 bail was more appropriate for organized crime suspects charged with murder.

The two attorneys could not even agree on the extent of Taylor's criminal background. Wisner claimed that Taylor had 13 arrests, five convictions and four pending charges. In the end Wisner won out and bail in the amount of $500,000 was placed on Thomas Taylor. (14)

Chapter 5
More Mad Dog Sullivan

'Mad Dog' Acquitted in Heist

Joseph "Mad Dog" Sullivan

On **June 25, 1982**, Joseph Sullivan was found not guilty of robbing a Marine Midland bank in Utica, N.Y. with a sawed off shotgun, which was the first charge that Sullivan stood trial for. Sullivan's co-defendant plead guilty to the charge and testified for the prosecution. Apparently the jury was convinced that the prosecution witness had sufficient reasons to lie and Sullivan was acquitted.

But Sullivan still faced a slew of charges, including a double homicide in Long Island for the murder of Virginia Carson and Richard Bretz in what police called a "drug related homicide," attempted murder charges for a June 8, 1981 assault of Brian Molese and Chris Crosthwaite in a Greenwich Village apartment, and murder and conspiracy charges for killing of John Fiorino, the Teamster Local #398 Vice-President. (15)

Following his acquittal in the bank heist, Sullivan was remanded to the Monroe County Jail where he was held in solitary confinement while he awaited his upcoming trial for the murder of John Fiorino.

Norton's Pub, located at 1730 N. Goodman St., was called "The Inferno" before being closed for organized crime ties. Dino Tortatice suffered a 24-inch gash while drinking there in July of 1982.

On **July 30, 1982,** Dino Tortatice suffered a 24-inch cut while drinking at a bar called The Inferno, located at 1730 N. Goodman Ave. According to police it was a clear message to Dino to back off. Dino was alleged to be the leader of what authorities described as a "Junior Mafia." He was supposedly involved in drug dealing, extortion, and prostitution. But Tortatice's friends denied all that. Instead, they said the group just sold drugs to each other and hung out at local bars.

According to Tommy Taylor, Dino's real problem was with Joey Tiraborelli, who was mistreating Dino's sister. Dino wasn't afraid of Joey and he refused to take any of Joey's shit.

The group was also alleged to be aligned with Thomas Pelusio, new leader of the C-Team faction, fighting for control of the Rochester Mafia. Members of the group denied that allegation as well, claiming to be friendly with members on both sides of the dispute. One member of Tortatice's group said,

"I know Tom Marotta pretty well. I used to sit on the porch and drink with him last summer at a friend's house. I would've gone and visited him in the hospital, but I didn't have time." (71)

Judge Denies Sullivan's Request
Cursing Sullivan Hauled from Court

Aug. 13, 1982 Democrat & Chronicle

Joseph Sullivan appeared before Monroe County Court Judge Eugene Bergin on **Aug. 12, 1982** in an unsuccessful attempt to be released from solitary confinement, a section of the prison nicknamed "The Box," where he was being held while awaiting trial for the murder of John Fiorino.

Normally prisoners were only sent to "the box" if they had physical or mental problems, if they disobeyed prison rules, or for "administrative reasons." Apparently Sullivan fell under the latter category, although prison officials refused to elaborate on the exact reason that Sullivan was continuously kept in solitary confinement after his arrest.

When Judge Bergin refused to allow Sullivan to be released from solitary confinement, Sullivan went off on the judge yelling, "This is all bullshit," and, "Is this a preview of what the trial will be like?"

As deputies dragged Sullivan out of the courtroom he continued yelling at the judge, comparing his case to the "Hammer Conspiracy." The "Hammer Conspiracies" was a book written by Frank Aloi that featured a scandal in the Monroe County Sheriff's Department, where deputies fabricated evidence in order to convict the hierarchy of organized crime in Rochester, N.Y. several years previously. (16)

Sullivan Says 'I'm No Hit Man'

Aug. 18, 1982 Democrat and Chronicle

Five days later, on **Aug. 17, 1982**, Joseph Sullivan granted an interview with the Democrat and Chronicle newspaper. It was the first of its kind since his arrest on Feb. 23, 1982. Sullivan admitted to reporters that he had killed before, but he denied being a "hit man" and he also denied killing John Fiorino.

Sullivan admitted he was in town on the December night in 1981 when Fiorino was killed, but he claimed to be at the Marriot Hotel in Greece when the murder occurred. He said he came to town (Rochester) to visit Thomas Taylor, a friend whom he played prison football with while at Attica Prison ten years prior.

Sullivan said he knew Louis DiGuilio and Thomas Torpey through his relationship with Taylor. Sully claimed, on the night of John Fiorino's murder at the Blue Gardenia Restaurant in Irondequoit, he let Louis DiGuilio borrow his car while he remained at the hotel in Greece. (17)

The New York Post ran this photo on page one the day after Sullivan's arrest. He and his girlfriend, Theresa Palmiere, are dressed like Bonnie and Clyde.

Sullivan's wife Gail told him after seeing this picture, "I thought I was your Bonnie!"

Joseph John Sullivan and Theresa Palmiere on the *New York Post's* front page.

Sullivan talked about his childhood, his family, his wife and his girlfriend. Joseph Sullivan was 43 years old at the time. By his own account he had spent about 25 of those years behind bars. Sullivan said he never had a girlfriend until he was released from prison at age 35 when he met Gail and got married.

Sullivan said he held a grudge on the FBI agents who apprehended him. He said they over-exaggerated his notoriety by comparing him to John Dillinger and Bonnie and Clyde, accusing him of so many murders just to make him sound more dangerous, and to make the "capture" more dramatic.

Chapter 6
Thomas Pelusio

Thomas Pelusio, C-Team member, entered into the Federal Witness Protection Program. He testified in Federal Court against several members of the Rochester Mafia, including Red Russotti and Rene Piccarreto.

Gerald Pelusio is Murdered in What Police Call a Case of Mistaken Identity

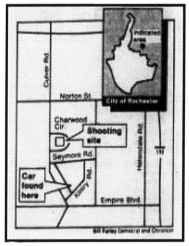

On **Aug. 27, 1982**, Gerald Pelusio and Bobby Comfort went to visit Bobby's brother, Pauly Comfort, who lived at 44 Charwood Circle in Irondequoit, N.Y. They arrived around 11:15 a.m.

As Paul Comfort opened the front door to his townhouse, a man in a green car drove up and fired an unknown number of shots through the passenger side window of the car from about 30 feet away. Several of those shots hit Gerald Pelusio.

Pelusio fell face down, face first in a bed of yellow and violet flowers on the left side of the concrete steps leading to the front door. He was shot three times, twice in the back, and once in the arm with a large caliber handgun.

Case of mistaken identity?

Police called the shooting a case of mistaken identity. Apparently the intended victim was Gerald's brother, Thomas. Sources said that the two men looked very much alike. Thomas Pelusio was a member of the insurgent group of organized crime figures, labeled the (C-Team), that was warring with the established faction of the Rochester Mafia headed by Rene Piccarreto and Samuel "Red" Russotti (A-Team). (18)

Gangland retaliation feared

Perinton man slain; police put on alert

[newspaper clipping]

Police feared there would be retaliation on A-Team members and ordered surveillance of known gambling establishments.

At 7 p.m. Friday, the same day of Pelusio's murder, gunshots were fired through a glass window on a building located at 7 Fernwood Ave. The building was a suspected gambling establishment, but it was unoccupied at the time of the shooting.

7 Fernwood Ave. in Rochester, N.Y. This building was the site of illegal gambling operations in the 1980's. The front windows were shot out on Aug. 27, 1982 by Thomas and Michael Pelusio after their brother, Gerald, was murdered earlier the same day.

About two hours later, a Rochester police officer stopped a vehicle with its headlights off on Laurelton Road containing three men. The men were identified as Michael and Thomas Pelusio and Raymond Sampson. A Mossberg 12-gauge shotgun loaded with five rounds of buckshot was found in the back seat of the car. The car was registered to Elaine Comfort, wife of Paul Comfort. All three men were arrested on weapons violations. (19)

According to the police, the warring between the Taylor and Torpey faction (C-Team) and the established Mob began when the insurgents became involved with narcotics.

> The warring between the Taylor and Torpey faction and the established mob began when the insurgent faction became involved in narcotics, police sources say.
>
> The Rochester underworld led by Piccaretto and Russotti is connected to illegal gambling establishments and never has been involved in drug operations on a large scale, sources say.

The established mob was linked to illegal gambling operations and never had been involved in drug operations on a large scale. Police said the warring continued in May of 1982 when Nicholas Mastrodonato was shot dead in a Gates coin shop. Mastrodonato was also linked to the Taylor and Torpey faction.

But according to Thomas Taylor, "This is all bullshit! Just some of the bullshit fed to Sgt. Grande by Thomas Marotta. Marotta was not going to mention the two real reasons for the C-Team, which were forcing Torpey to pay the "vig" and me scarring Joey Tiraborrelli for life in front of his friends."

Pelusio leads mob faction?
Police: Slain man's brother is chief of insurgent group

Police had questioned more than 200 people in connection with the Pelusio slaying. Irondequoit police headed the investigation with help from the city Police Department's Organized Crime Task Force, the Monroe County Sheriff's Department, the Monroe County district attorney's office, the state police, and the FBI. [20]

Thomas Pelusio Leads Mob Faction (C-Team)
Police Say Slain Man's Brother is Chief of Insurgent Group

Thomas Pelusio

Thomas Pelusio allegedly became the insurgent faction's leader when Thomas Torpey and Thomas Taylor were jailed on June 8, 1982 in connection with the Dec. 17, 1981 shotgun slaying of union leader John Fiorino, according to newspapers and the police.

Pelusio also took over the operation of a suspected gambling establishment on St. Paul Street, once controlled by Torpey, when Torpey and Taylor were arrested, police sources stated. But police surveillance of the St. Paul Street parlor disclosed that business had slumped considerably when Pelusio took over. Thomas Pelusio was also involved in his family's business, Rochester Linoleum and Carpet Center, police said.

Although police could only speculate as to the role Thomas Pelusio played in the mob wars, one fact remained, there was little doubt that Thomas Pelusio's association with the C-Team cost his brother his life.

But according to Thomas Taylor, Bobby Comfort was the real leader of the C-Team following their arrest (Torpey and Taylor). Pelusio was used as a front man to take the heat. But instead of absorbing the heat, Thomas Pelusio and his brother Mike Pelusio both entered into the Federal Witness Protection Program and testified against the Rochester Mob in Federal Court.

Bobby Comfort (above) became the leader of the C-Team after Torpey and Taylor's arrest for murder.

Chapter 7
Sullivan's Murder Trial

Joseph Sullivan's Murder Trial Begins

Joseph Sullivan's murder trial began on Sept. 9, 1982.

On **Sept. 9, 1982,** Joseph Sullivan's murder trial began. Defense Lawyer Anthony F. Leonardo Jr. claimed that the entire case hinged on the testimony of Louis DiGuilio, who originally was Sullivan's co-defendant, and also charged with murder.

Although DiGuilio was caught driving the murder vehicle, the car itself was owned by and registered to Joseph Sullivan. The license plates had fake plates directly over the top of the real ones. Inside of the trunk of the car police found a very large sum of money and a silencer for a gun.

Nonetheless, Anthony Leonardo, Sullivan's attorney, spent the day emphasizing DiGuilio's role in the murder and the deal he cut with the state to save his own ass from life in prison, or worse. (21)

Some time before DiGuilio's trial started and the jury was being selected, DiGuilio became an informant, or a witness for the state. In exchange for his testimony, DiGuilio was allowed to plead guilty to a lesser charge and he was to be sentenced the following month, on Oct. 12, 1982. He was eventually placed into the Witness Protection Program.

Sullivan's Girlfriend Fails to Show in Court

Theresa Palmiere

The following day, on **Sept. 10, 1982**, the second day of the trial, the judge ordered an arrest warrant for Theresa Palmiere. Palmiere, who was arrested with Sullivan, was scheduled to testify at Sullivan's trial but she failed to show up for court.

Palmiere was allegedly supposed to testify about comments that Joseph Sullivan made to her immediately following the murder of John Fiorino. According to the Assistant District Attorney, those comments would directly link Sullivan to the murder. When Joe made it back to New York City and visited Theresa following the Fiorino murder, he had allegedly said to her, "I got shot up in Rochester."

Earlier that day a woman named Maria Sands testified that the car identified as the murder car was registered to her. She was Gail Sullivan's best friend. She claimed she was just helping a friend. Her and Gail, Sullivan's wife, were like sisters, she said.

When Sands was first shown a picture of the car and was asked by the Assistant District Attorney if she recognized it, Sands was clearly agitated and nearly in tears. She said she could not remember. At that point, Sullivan spoke up. "They know its my car, relax," as he made a calming gesture with his hand toward Sands. As she left the witness stand she turned toward Sullivan and smiled. Sullivan smiled back at her. (22)

DiGiulio Testifies at Sullivan's Trial
Tells of Stalking Victims, Drugs and Death

On **Sept. 14, 1982**, Louis DiGuilio, driver of the getaway car turned informant, testified in court against Joseph Sullivan. He told a story of snorting cocaine with Joseph Sullivan, Thomas Torpey, and Thomas Taylor while plotting the assassination of Richard Marino, Underboss of the Rochester Mafia and John Fiorino, a Captain or Capo of the same organization.

Sullivan and DiGiulio held the contract for the killing and Torpey and Taylor had hired them. The plan entailed driving around the streets of Rochester, cruising the local bars looking for their victims. Torpey and Taylor were in one car and DiGiulio and Sullivan were in another car. It took two days of searching before they finally located Fiorino. (23)

Same article on the same day, only the headline was different.

Sullivan Berates Prosecutor

Joseph Sullivan

Louis DiGiulio continued his testimony the following day on **Sept. 15, 1982**. His testimony lasted well into the afternoon. He described the assassination plot in the Marriot Hotel in Greece on Dec. 15, 1981. There was talk about how the regular Mafia didn't deserve to run the city and about how the four men each would receive "a piece of the city" after killing John Fiorino and Dick Marino.

The last witness called that day was Don Felter, a Marriott Hotel Employee. The prosecutor asked him a series of questions about a man named Victor Weiner. The last question he asked Felter was, "Do you know whether Victor Weiner is alive or dead?" That question caused Joseph Sullivan, who had behaved all day, to have a sudden outburst and Sullivan began yelling at the prosecutor.

Sullivan accused the prosecutor of putting on a charade by enticing testimony from witnesses that implied that a man that Joseph Sullivan knew was now dead. Three times the prosecutor implied the man was dead. "You want to know who Vic Weiner is, ask my wife," Sullivan said as he pointed toward his wife Gail. The man was Gail Sullivan's brother and he was not dead.

Deputies immediately surrounded Sullivan, who was clearly agitated. "Get off me," he spewed at the deputies, "I'll sit down." The reason for the specific line of questioning never was determined, nor was the reason for Sullivan's agitation to the questions. (24)

Sullivan Case Rests, Sullivan Never Called to Testify

Joseph Sullivan's murder trial came to an end on **Sept. 20, 1982**, as both sides gave closing arguments. Sullivan was never called to the witness stand to testify on his own behalf. Sullivan's attorney, Anthony Leonardo*, felt the state failed to prove its case and Sullivan's testimony would not be necessary. (25)

Sullivan Found Guilty

'

After two long days of jury deliberations, Joseph Sullivan was found guilty and convicted on **Sept. 23, 1982** of the murder of John Fiorino. He faced 25 years to life in prison. (26)

---

* Anthony Leonardo, the famous Rochester attorney, would later be found guilty of money laundering and cocaine distribution, and he was sentenced to prison.

'Mad Dog' Sullivan Draws
25 Years to Life for Murder Rap

On **Oct. 7, 1982**, Joseph Sullivan received the maximum sentence of 25 years to life for the shotgun slaying of John Fiorino. Although he planned to file an appeal, he still faced trial in Suffolk County for killing two people and wounding a third person. He was still a suspect in multiple other murders as well.

The previous day, Oct. 6, 1982, Theresa Palmiere was indicted by a grand jury for second degree criminal contempt for failing to appear as a witness and testify during the course of Sullivan's 17 day murder trial. Palmiere's previous testimony to a grand jury in February of 1982 was read to the court.

Her testimony elicited the fact that Sullivan had fled to New York City after the Dec. 17, 1981 murder of Fiorino. Sullivan met up with Theresa Palmiere on Dec. 23, 1981 and told her he got "shot up" a few days before. They met up because Sullivan wanted to see Palmiere's child, which he was the father of.
(27)

Sullivan Under 24 Hour Guard

Joseph Sullivan was placed in isolation on Oct. 13, 1982 following reports of an attempted escape.

Joseph Sullivan was placed in isolation on **Oct. 13, 1982** while he was in the Suffolk County Jail, and following reports of an attempted escape. But Sheriff John P. Finnerty said, "Sullivan isn't going anywhere." He was placed on 24 hour guard.

Sullivan and his co-defendant, Marko Tedesco, were waiting to be tried on murder charges for killing Richard Bretz, 35, and Virginia Carson, 25, the previous year in Centerreach.

Two men came to visit Tedesco in jail using fake names and attempted to smuggle two .38 caliber bullets to him in an unopened box of Kleenex. Police believe the bullets were intended for Sullivan, who planned to use them in an escape attempt.

Sullivan had been taken to Attica for processing the day after his sentencing, and while there one of the guards overheard Sullivan claim that he was going to escape from the Suffolk County Jail, which was where he was headed next. The guard alerted Sheriff Finnerty of the Suffolk County Jail, who went on high alert. The escape plot was foiled.

In 1971, Sullivan became the only man to successfully escape from Attica State Prison. Before that Sullivan had also escaped from the federal detention facility on Governor's Island in New York City and from a mental hospital in Trenton, N.J. (28)

Chapter 8
Shootings

Mob Figures Indicted on Weapons Charges

3 mob figures indicted on weapons charges

Thomas Pelusio arraigned here; two others being held in Boston

By Jody McPhillips
Democrat and Chronicle

A federal grand jury in Rochester has indicted three reputed underworld figures on weapons charges stemming from an incident Aug. 27.

Arraigned yesterday in Rochester on those federal charges was Thomas A. Pelusio, 36, of 96 Laurelton Road. Thomas Pelusio pleaded not guilty to federal charges of unlawful possession of a 12-gauge shotgun and ammunition at his arraignment in U.S. District Court, the day after the grand jury indictments were made public.

He was released on $5,000 bail.

His brother Michael Pelusio, 28, of 540 Lake Ave., and Raymond Sampson, 47, of 722 Broad St., will be arraigned on the same federal charges in Rochester next week. They were arrested in Boston Saturday on the same charges and are in federal custody there in lieu of $100,000 bail.

All three men had been arraigned on similar state weapons charges in Monroe County Court in connection with the same incident and were out on bail at the time of their federal indictments.

If convicted on the federal charges, they could face up to five years in jail and a $5,000 fine, or both.

Police say all three men have ties to an insurgent faction in the Rochester underworld formerly led by Thomas E. Taylor and Thomas M. Torpey. Taylor and Torpey are in Monroe County jail, awaiting trial on charges of killing reputed Mafia figure John Fiorino last December.

Last Aug. 27, a third Pelusio brother, Gerald, of 25 Heatherwood Road, Parlexton, was slain by a gunman in front of a townhouse at 44 Charwood Circle, Irondequoit.

Police theorize Gerald Pelusio, whose ties to organized crime are said to be minor, was killed by mistake and that the true target was his lookalike brother Thomas.

The slaying of Gerald Pelusio is thought to have been in retaliation for a "confrontation" a month earlier between Thomas Pelusio, Michael Pelusio and Rene Piccarreto, reputed leader of the established Mafia that the Taylor-Torpey faction was challenging.

Hours after Gerald Pelusio was slain, police stopped a 1976 tan and white Buick on Laurelton Road after the car's lights were turned off as police approached.

Police had been investigating shots that were fired through the front window of 7 Fernwood Ave. at 7 p.m. that night, apparently in retribution for Gerald Pelusio's slaying. The building, which was not occupied at the time, was a suspected gambling operation controlled by the established underworld, police said.

Inside the car were the two Pelusio brothers and Sampson, a convicted felon who also has ties to the insurgent faction.

Police found a loaded Mossberg 12-gauge pump-action shotgun on the back seat. It is illegal for convicted felons to own weapons.

Oct. 20, 1982 Democrat and Chronicle

On **Oct. 19, 1982**, a six-count indictment was filed against Michael A. Pelusio, Thomas A. Pelusio, and Raymond Sampson, charging each with two counts of unlawful receipt of a firearm and unlawful receipt of ammunition in violation of 18 U.S.C. Secs. 922(h)(1), 924(a) and 2.1.

Sampson's case was severed by the district court prior to trial. Motions by Michael and Thomas to suppress evidence of the seizure of the firearm and ammunition as violative of their Fourth Amendment rights were denied by Judge Telesca after an extended evidentiary hearing.

Michael A. Pelusio (Michael) and Thomas A. Pelusio (Thomas) were both found guilty. Judge Michael A. Telesca, convicted them of unlawful receipt of firearms and ammunition transported in interstate commerce. Michael was convicted of one count charging receipt of a gun and another charging receipt of ammunition, while under felony indictment and while having previously been convicted of a felony.

Thomas was likewise convicted on two counts, charging unlawful receipt of the gun and ammunition while under indictment for a felony. The Court affirmed their convictions of unlawful receipt of the gun and reversed their convictions of unlawful receipt of the ammunition. (29)

Mad Dog Sullivan Found Guilty of Killing Two Junkies

Nov. 25, 1982 Daily News, New York, N.Y.

On **Nov. 24, 1982**, Joseph Sullivan was found guilty of murdering Richard Bretz and Virginia Carson, two junkies, in Seldon, L.I. on Dec. 8, 1981. He was also found guilty of the attempted murder of Andrew Soldo. Soldo had been shot in the head and stabbed in the neck, but he survived and became the prosecution's main witness.

According to Soldo, the trio was attempting to purchase an ounce of cocaine from Sullivan and Marko Tedesco, Sullivan's co-defendant, for $2,300. They all met in Soldo's apartment, waiting for Sullivan and Tedesco to arrive.

Sullivan suddenly burst into the apartment and shot all three of the occupants in the head. He then turned to Marko Tedesco and said, "Cut them. Make sure they're dead."

Tedesco then slit the throats of all three victims before fleeing with Sullivan and the $2,300.

Following a seven day trial, Sullivan and Tedesco appeared in court in handcuffs and leg irons to hear the verdict. Both men had been found guilty of four counts of murder and they each faced 120 years in prison. Sullivan still faced yet another murder trial for killing two men in Manhattan in July of 1981. (30)

Rochester Mafia 'Captain' Thomas Marotta is Shot Six Times

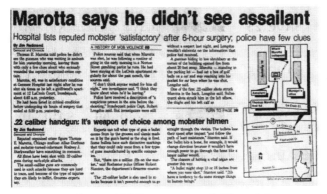

April 13, 1983 Democrat and Chronicle

Meanwhile, back in Rochester, Mafia "Captain" Thomas Marotta was shot six times on **April 12, 1983** with a .22 caliber handgun. Marotta, who survived the attack, was shot at 4:40 a.m. after he left his girlfriend's apartment on La Croix Circle in Irondequoit, N.Y.

Thomas Marotta ran a gambling parlor on Norton Street at the time. Police suspected that Marotta was shot while following his regular routine of going in for an early visit to that gambling parlor.
(31)

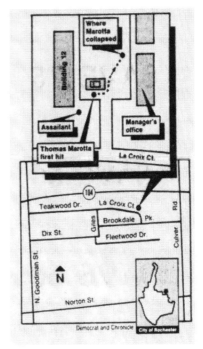

Location of April 12, 1983 Marotta shooting.

Dino Tortatice was then roughed up on **April 22, 1983** by the A-Team while drinking with some friends inside a bar called DJ's Lounge, located at 1700 Clifford Ave. The friends said they used to drink at a bar called "The Inferno," which was right down

1700 Clifford Ave. location of former DJ's Lounge owned by John Travigno, Rochester Mafia Soldier in the early 1980's. Dino Tortatice was roughed with "blackjacks" by members of the A-Team on April 22, 1983 inside the bar.

the street, but they don't go there anymore out of respect for Dino, since he was assaulted there.

DJ's Lounge was owned by John Travigno, a Rochester Mafia Soldier. A-Team members were attempting to get Dino to admit to shooting Thomas Marotta by beating a confession out of him with blackjacks. They apparently did not know at the time that the shooting was actually ordered by A-Team leaders Rene Piccarreto and Red Russotti. Marotta was the #4 man in the Rochester Mafia after Russotti, Piccarreto, and Richard Marino.

Dino Tortatice, age 24, was eventually murdered in front of his mother's home while sitting on the front porch with friends on **Aug. 2, 1983.** (32) In between those two events, the trial for the 44 Club incident began and ended. Thomas Taylor, Thomas Pelusio and his brother, Michael Pelusio, were all convicted of assaulting Moe Alaimo. Dino's brother, Rocky, eventually married Sammy G.'s daughter, Gina.

Assault Trial of 3 Reputed Mobsters for 44 Club Incident
Three Men Give Conflicting Testimony

The assault trial of Thomas Taylor, Michael Pelusio and Thomas Pelusio for beating "Moe" Alaimo at the "44 Club" in March of 1982 began on **June 29, 1983**. The three men were accused of beating Alaimo with a broomstick and punching and kicking him.

On the second day of the trial, three "witnesses" to the alleged attack each took the witness stand and told conflicting stories as to what transpired that evening.

One witness denied that card games ever took place at the club, despite evidence to the contrary including the testimony of Moe Alaimo himself. Another witness testified that he was "unconscious" during the entire 25 minute beating and never saw a thing. A third witness was only able to identify one of the defendants as being one of the five men that entered the club together on the night of the alleged beating. He then identified the same man's attorney as being another of the five men.

Robert Collins was the doorman at the Caserta Political and Social Club located at 44 Lake Ave. in Rochester. The club was commonly known as the "44 Club" and was a known gambling establishment. He testified that Moe Alaimo ran the club and handled the money. He claimed to have seen as much as $10,000 at a time in Moe's possession.

Moe testified that he was only paid $50 a day to run the games. He further testified that it was Charles Russo that ran the games at the 44 Club. Charles Russo testified that he was unconscious the entire time and never saw anything. (58)

Assault Trial of 3 Reputed Mobsters Goes to Jury

The assault trial came to a close on **July 6, 1983**. Lawyers gave their closing statements. Both sides said the case boiled down to which witnesses told the most believable story.

Moe Alaimo had testified that Thomas Taylor kicked him continuously for 25 straight minutes while the other men beat him with a broomstick and kicked and punched him. Taylor's lawyer, John Speranza, ridiculed that version of events. Speranza made Taylor, who was 6' tall and weighed roughly 225 lbs. stand up for the jury.

Quite frankly he said, "**If my client kicked anybody for 25 minutes, he'd be dead!**"

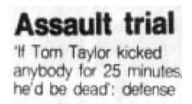

Thomas Torpey was also there with Taylor and the Pelusio brothers that evening. Charlie Russo and Thomas Taylor were arguing over something to do with the card game and they grabbed each other and fell to the floor. Then Moe Alaimo attacked Taylor with a broom handle. The Pelusio's grabbed the broomstick away from Alaimo and struck Alaimo once or twice in defense of Taylor.

Moe Alaimo kept mumbling, "Marrota's going to take care of this, you haven't heard the end of this." Thomas Marotta was described by police as a "Captain" in the Rochester Mafia at the time on the "A-Team." (59)

Guilty Verdicts for Pelusio and Taylor

Guilty verdicts for Pelusios and Taylor

A state Supreme Court jury last night convicted three reputed mobsters of assault charges in connection with the March 12, 1982, beating of a man in a gambling parlor.

State Supreme Court Justice David O. Boehm set sentencing for Aug. 16.

Thomas E. Taylor, 42; Thomas A. Pelusio, 36; and his brother Michael A. Pelusio, 28; were found guilty of second-degree assault after the jury deliberated for nearly 12 hours. The verdict was returned at 11:47 p.m.

The three men were stoic, but the Pelusios' mother, one of about 15 people who had waited all night in the courtroom, shook her head and put her hands to her face.

July 7, 1983

Despite all of the conflicting testimony about what actually occurred on the night of March 12, 1982 and the parade of "less than credible" witnesses during the trial, a state Supreme Court jury convicted Thomas E. Taylor, 42; Thomas A. Pelusio, 36; and his brother Michael A. Pelusio, 28, of assault charges on **July 6, 1983**.

All three men were found guilty of second degree assault in connection with the March 12, 1982 beating of Samuel "Moe" Alaimo inside a Rochester Mafia A-Team controlled gambling parlor called the "44 Club," located at 44 Lake Ave. The jury deliberated for nearly 12 hours before returning the guilty verdict.

Thomas Taylor and Michael Pelusio remained free on bail pending appeals. Thomas Pelusio's bail had been revoked the month prior and he was immediately taken from the courtroom in handcuffs. (60)

Dino Tortatice is Murdered

Aug. 4, 1983 Democrat and Chronicle

On **Aug. 2, 1983**, Dino Tortatice, 24, was gunned down outside of his mother's home on Norran Drive in the northern part of Rochester, N.Y. Tortatice had a reputation for being a "tough guy." He led a gang of 10 to 15 young men, who would shake down bar owners for money and threaten others that got in their way. Some called them a junior mob.

Police speculated that this kind of ambition is what led to his death. An assassin unloaded an automatic weapon on Tortatice as he sat outside his mother's home drinking a beer. Dino Tortatice died less than an hour later. He was the third recent homicide victim, associated with an insurgent faction of the Rochester Mafia called the "C-Team." Police at the time were investigating similarities in the Mastrodonato and Pelusio murders. (32)

But the police theory was merely speculation. Thomas Taylor, the original leader of the C-Team, when asked about Dino, stated, "Dino had nothing to do with us."

Two Men Receive 2 to 6 Year Terms for Assault Convictions the Other Gets 2 and 1/2 to 5 Years

On **Aug. 16, 1983**, Thomas and Michael Pelusio were both sentenced to two to six years in prison for their assault convictions for the March 1982 beating of Moe Alaimo inside of the 44 Club. Thomas E. Taylor, also convicted, had his sentencing delayed due to legal challenges.

The prosecution wanted Taylor to be sentenced as a second felony offender, which would result in a more severe penalty. But Taylor's defense lawyer insisted that the prosecution prove that his client was the same Thomas E. Taylor that was convicted of conspiracy and extortion in 1964.

Eventually, on Aug. 3, 1984 Thomas E. Taylor was sentenced to two and one-half to five years in state prison for his role in the assault. Taylor was allowed to remain free on previously posted $200,000 bail pending an appeal. (61)

Marotta gunned down again

Thomas E. Marotta

Three months after the Tortatice murder, on **Nov. 10, 1983**, reputed organized crime "Captain" Thomas E. Marotta was shot for the second time in less than a year. Police at the time thought that the shooting was in retaliation for the Aug. 2, 1983 murder of Dino Tortatice.

Police also thought that the Tortatice killing may have been retribution for an attempt on Marotta's life the previous April.

Toni Tortatice said her brother, Dino, 24, was killed after established mob leaders read in newspaper articles that he and a group of friends had been extensively questioned by police in the first Marotta shooting. She was afraid of retaliation on her younger brother.

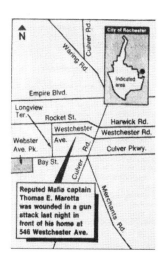

Toni vividly remembered watching her older brother, Dino, gunned down the previous August in front of their parents' Norran Drive home. She feared her younger brother, Rocco, could also die, as violent attacks were exchanged by rival local mob factions. Both brothers grew up tough and street-wise, Toni Tortatice said, but neither had been involved with organized crime. (33)

Men Questioned After Marotta Shooting

Democrat and Chronicle Nov. 12, 1983

On the night Marotta was shot, two men were arrested near the reputed underworld leader's house at 546 Westchester Ave., Irondequoit. Irondequoit police arrested the men 30 minutes after Marotta was shot in his driveway at 11:45 p.m.

Frederick Kelch, 238 Milford St., and Timothy Hartwigh, 27, of 47 Child St., were scheduled to appear at a later date in Irondequoit Court to answer the weapons charge; they were charged with criminal possession of a dangerous weapon (dagger) after being caught near Marotta's house. Marotta, 41, was said by local authorities to be fourth in command of the Rochester Organized Crime Family.

Marotta was in fair condition, the day after the shooting, at Genesee Hospital, a hospital spokeswoman said. He was struck at least three times in the chest in an ambush attack by an unidentified assailant who emptied a small-caliber handgun, missing several times, said Irondequoit police Capt. Robert Longdue. It was the second attempt on Marotta's life in seven months. On April 12, 1983, Marotta was shot six times by a gunman in the parking lot of an apartment building at La Croix Court in Irondequoit.

No one had been charged in either shooting, but Irondequoit police and members of the countywide Organized Crime

Task Force say they were investigating similarities in the shootings. Some organized crime investigators theorize the latest Marotta shooting was in retaliation for the Aug. 2, 1983 slaying of gang leader Dino Tortatice, 24, of Norran Drive. The Tortatice shooting, investigators have said, was suspected to have been in retaliation for the first attempt on Marotta's life. "It's been a see-saw battle," one detective said.

The gunman stepped out from behind Marotta's house and fired from about eight feet away as Marotta was getting into a late-model Oldsmobile. The gunman then ran behind the house in a northeasterly direction toward the intersection of Whittington and Harwick Roads, hopping two or three backyard fences.

"It's not clear whether a getaway vehicle was involved." Marotta's wife, Mary, told police she watched her husband fall, then saw the gunman flee. The only description she could provide of the assailant was that he was about six feet tall.

It would later be discovered that a "hitman" for the "A-Team" of the Rochester Mafia, Dominic Taddeo, was the person who murdered Dino Tortatice right outside of his house on Aug. 2, 1983.

Dominic Taddeo

> Dominic Taddeo was a "hit-man" for the A-Team of the Rochester Mafia. He committed three murders and two attempted murders.

"Red" Russotti, the "Boss" of the "A Team", ordered the extermination of all "C Team" members involved in the Fiorino murder. Tortatice was not even a C-Team member, according to Thomas Taylor, the C-Team leader. Oddly enough, it would later be discovered that Dominic Taddeo was also responsible for the Marotta shootings. He would eventually admit to them all. He was the "A Team's" "one man house cleaner."

Police said Tortatice had led a gang of about a dozen Irondequoit and eastside Rochester men, including Kelch and Hartwigh, who tried to run a small-time racketeering operation. None had been charged or convicted of racketeering. Tortatice and the others were questioned by a federal grand jury in Rochester investigating the first Marotta shooting and local racketeering.

The results of the investigation were not made public. Gang members interviewed in Democrat and Chronicle articles after the first attack on Marotta pointed out the ambush-style and the "amateurish" manner of the shootings.

The shooting of Marotta, came a year and a day after Marotta and nine others were indicted by a federal grand jury in Rochester on racketeering charges. The 10 were still awaiting trial at the time.

Investigators said the Tortatice gang was the third succession of an insurgent faction of mobsters warring with Rochester's established organized Crime Family for control of local rackets. (The C-Team) The insurgents were first led by reputed mobsters Thomas A. Taylor and Thomas M. Torpey, who were then on trial in Monroe County Court in connection with the December 1981 shotgun slaying of union leader and mob "Underboss" John N. Fiorino. (34)

When Thomas Torpey and Thomas Taylor were jailed for the Fiorino murder, control of the C-Team was passed on to Thomas Pelusio. Then when Pelusio was jailed on weapons charges, leadership of the insurgent faction of the Rochester Mafia (C-Team) was allegedly passed to Dino Tortatice.

It was later pointed out by C-Team leader Thomas Taylor that Dino Tortatice had nothing at all to do with the C-Team. Dino's real beef was with Mafia Soldier Joey Tiraborelli, who was mistreating Dino's sister, according to Taylor.

Chapter 9
Torpey and Taylor's Murder Trials

The Trials

Torpey and Taylor's Murder Trial

Nov. 16, 1983 Democrat and Chronicle

After the conclusion of Joe Sullivan's trial for the murder of John Fiorino, the trial for Sullivan's co-defendants, Thomas Taylor and Thomas Torpey began.

Police officer Michael DiGiovanni, the Irondequoit police officer who arrested Louis DiGuilio and was shot at by Joseph Sullivan, was among the first witnesses to testify for the prosecution.

Policeman Tells of His Close Call on Night Fiorino Slain

Irondequoit police Officer Michael DiGiovanni testified on **Nov. 15, 1983** about Fiorino's murder. He said he remembered the night of Dec. 17, 1981 very well. He was on routine patrol that snowy night when he spotted a light colored Cadillac with its headlights out skid into a snowbank near the intersection of Helendale Road. DiGiovanni said he thought he'd witnessed a drunk driving accident, but that thought soon changed.

As he approached the intersection, a man in a wide brimmed hat stepped out of the Cadillac; DiGiovanni said he remembered making eye contact with Sullivan as he emerged from the passenger door with a long gun in his hands. Sullivan crouched, leveled a sawed-off shot gun at him, and fired several shots in rapid succession, DiGiovanni testified.

Lt. Michael DiGiovanni

"**I kicked open my car door and as I came out he was firing at me,**" he said. "**I counted three [shots].**"

As the blasts shattered the windshield of his patrol car, DiGiovanni said he fired two or three quick shots from his own revolver before moving to close the distance between him and Sullivan.

"**I popped the rest of the rounds out and I saw him lurch forward so I knew I hit him,**" DiGiovanni said. "**I went down, reloaded my gun, came back up, and he was gone.**"

Then, once other police and sheriff deputies arrived, we tracked Louis DiGiulio, the driver, by the footprints he'd left in the snow. The tracks led to a school on Helendale Road. "We caught him in the bushes," DiGiovanni said. (35)

DiGiovanni said DiGuilio was laying face down with his hands under his body.

> "I put the barrel of the shotgun in the side of his neck and I told him if he moved I would shoot him."

Informant Tells of Bitterness Between Torpey and the Rochester Mob

On **Nov. 16, 1983**, the fifth day of testimony at the murder trial of Thomas Taylor and Thomas Torpey, murder suspect turned informant Louis DiGiulio testified that he recalled that tension and bitterness had festered between Torpey and the Rochester Mob.

DiGiulio described his relationship to Torpey and Taylor and "reputed members of the local Mob." He told of illegal gambling joints, payoffs, backroom meetings and threats among organized crime figures. DiGiulio also testified that he attended a meeting between Torpey and Taylor and the leaders of the Rochester Mafia at Torpey's joint on Lyell Avenue.

He testified that Rene Piccarreto, Samuel "Red" Russotti, Thomas Torpey, Thomas Taylor and himself were present, although he watched the meeting from the bar.

Then two weeks before Fiorino was murdered on Dec. 17, 1981, he (Fiorino) walked into Torpey's joint looking "kinda mad" DiGiulio said.

Thomas Torpey

"John what brings you here," DiGiulio said he asked Fiorino.

"Torpey ain't paying, I am here to close this place down," Fiorino responded.

When Torpey walked in to the bar, Fiorino confronted him saying, **"You're causing trouble in this town. I want to avoid another war. I will give you the $350 a week, just say you'll pay!"**

But Fiorino's efforts were rebuffed. Torpey was adamant in his refusal to pay the "vig" on his joint. Before leaving, Fiorino turned to Torpey and said, **"You're no superman. You can bleed and die like everyone else."** (36)

You Put the Finger of Death on Fiorino, Defense Lawyer Tells Witness

As testimony continued the following day, **Nov. 17, 1983**, the defense attorney for Torpey and Taylor tore into the prosecution's star witness, Louis DiGiulio, who was testifying for his second day. It was an effort to discredit him and prove that he was lying to save his own skin.

DiGiulio testified that Torpey and Taylor had hired professional hit-man Joseph Sullivan to kill Fiorino because they wanted to take over Rochester. DiGiulio said Torpey called the Mob "a bunch of punks" and said that they did not deserve to run the town.

Torpey just outright refused to continue paying the "vig" on his joint, saying, "I helped them take this town. Why should I pay?"

But, Defense Attorney John F. Speranza was ruthless. (37)

"John Fiorino was a pal of yours," lawyer John F. Speranza said to DiGiulio. "You put the finger of death on him. You knew that those flaming bits of metal from that shotgun would blow through John Fiorino's head like a ripe tomato."

Nov. 18, 1983 Democrat and Chronicle

The statement was an effort by Speranza to discredit Louis DiGiulio in front of the jury and show them (the jury) that DiGiulio willingly participated in the crime and that he had his own motives for doing so.

The Gospel According to Louie

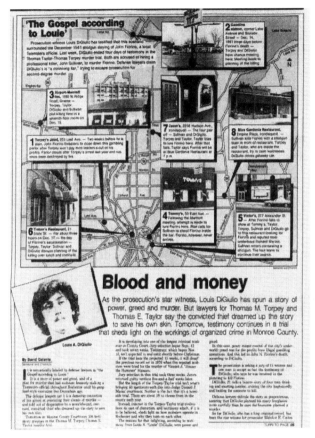

Nov. 27, 1983 Democrat and Chronicle

Of course Louis DiGiulio's testimony was self-serving. DiGiulio was a participant in the murder and he faced a life sentence or worse. In exchange for testifying against his co-conspirators, DiGiulio was granted a lighter prison sentence. He was also placed into the Federal Witness Protection Program. (38)

Lawyer Claims Judges Ruling Blocked Sullivan from Clearing Torpey

Dec. 2, 1983 Democrat and Chronicle

The Court refused to grant immunity to convicted killer Joseph Sullivan, allowing him to testify in the Torpey and Taylor murder trial. He was called to testify by the prosecution. Sullivan claimed that he had no choice but to invoke his right to the 5th Amendment and failed to testify because his testimony may have been self incriminating.

Thomas Torpey's lawyer, Felix Lapine, claimed that Sullivan could have provided testimony proving that Torpey was innocent. Sullivan's lawyer, Anthony Leonardo Jr., stated that Sullivan will not answer any questions related to the Fiorino murder because appeals were pending in that case. (39)

Fiorino's Widow Takes the Witness Stand

Fiorino's widow, on stand, recalls last hour she spent with husband

By David Galante
Democrat and Chronicle

The widow of slain Teamsters official John N. Fiorino took the witness stand yesterday in the murder trial of Thomas M. Torpey and Thomas E. Taylor, recalling the last hour she spent with her husband.

Lida Fiorino testified briefly, not looking at the two men accused of plotting her husband's death. Fiorino was the vice president and paid business agent of Teamsters Local 398.

Mrs. Fiorino told the Monroe County Court jury of 11 women and one man that on Dec. 17, 1981, her husband, dressed in a business suit, came home from work about 5:30 p.m.

"We talked for a few minutes," she said. "He changed his clothes. Then he went to lie down on the couch."

Mrs. Fiorino and her husband had planned a quiet evening together at their home on Venice Circle in Irondequoit, she said.

Mrs. Fiorino said her husband made a telephone call about 6 p.m. "It was just a friendly conversation," she said. Her husband then received a couple of calls and talked on the phone until about 6:15 p.m., she said.

Mrs. Fiorino testified that her husband left their house about 6:25, telling her he was going to the Blue Gardenia Restaurant. The prosecution says Fiorino, a reputed

Thomas Torpey **Thomas Taylor**

organized-crime figure, then drove to the Blue Gardenia, where he was shot and killed about 6:45 p.m. in the parking lot near the restaurant's front entrance by a professional hit man wielding a sawed-off shotgun.

The trigger man, Joseph John Sullivan of New York City, was convicted last year of second-degree murder in connection with the Fiorino slaying.

Torpey and Taylor are accused of hiring Sullivan to kill Fiorino as a signal to mob leaders that a new circle of organized-crime figures was moving in on the Rochester rackets.

Also yesterday, a prosecution witness apparently took prosecutor Melchor E. Castro by surprise when he changed the testimony he gave during Sullivan's trial.

TURN TO PAGE 2B

Dec. 9, 1983
Democrat and Chronicle

On **Dec. 8, 1983**, the widow of murdered Teamsters Local #398 Vice-President John Fiorino took the witness stand and testified at the trial of Thomas Torpey and Thomas Taylor.

Lida Fiorino testified that her husband John received a phone call on Dec. 17, 1981 at about 6 p.m., on the night he died. After hanging up the phone John told her that he was going to the Blue Gardenia Restaurant to meet "The Eagle." "The Eagle" was Thomas Taylor's nickname.

Lida Fiorino testified that her husband left the house at about 6:25 p.m. Twenty minutes later, at 6:45, Fiorino was shot dead in the parking lot of the Blue Gardenia. (40)

The Prosecution Rests

The prosecution rested its case the following day, on Dec. 9, 1983. The defense began calling witnesses. Marvin Pizzo was the fifth witness to take the stand for the defense. He was a long time friend of Thomas Torpey. During Pizzo's testimony, Prosecutor Melchor E. Castro had a sudden outburst in the courtroom after the judge scolded him and ruled that his line of questioning was "out of order."

In an effort to discredit the witness, the prosecutor asked Pizzo if he knew Frank Valenti, the former Rochester Mafia Boss. When defense lawyer Felix LaPine objected, the prosecutor complained that **"the defense was putting perjurers on the stand, one after the other."** The judge scolded Castro for his remark and instructed the jury to disregard it.

Pizzo testified that he called the Blue Gardenia on the night of the shooting to see if his friend Ben Manning, owner of the Blue Gardenia, was alright. He had mistakenly heard that Manning was killed. After telling Pizzo that Manning was okay, Torpey asked Pizzo to come to the Blue Gardenia because he and Thomas Taylor needed a ride.

Pizzo testified that when he arrived he parked next door at Star Market Supermarket. "There was all kinds of turmoil, police officers everywhere," he said. I heard a detective shout, **"Hey Taylor, get your car out of that fire zone."**

Taylor responded back to the detective by saying,

"You get in the car, start it, if it doesn't blow up (because of a car bomb) I'll get it. If not I'm going with Marvin Pizzo."

"They never did call the bomb squad to check the car, so I left it there," Taylor said.

Jan. 3, 1984 Democrat and Chronicle

The Torpey-Taylor murder trial was Monroe County's longest and costliest trial in its history. It ended in a mistrial, jurors being hopelessly deadlocked. Judge Donald J. Mark declared a mistrial on **Jan. 2, 1984**, when jurors could not reach a verdict after six days of deliberation. The trial itself lasted for three and a half months. The Monroe County District Attorney said that he would seek a new trial, possibly outside of Monroe County. (41)

Pictured at left are Joe Sullivan, Thomas Taylor, and Thomas Torpey. Their murder trial for killing John Fiorino became the longest trial in Monroe County history, lasting three and a half months.

Thomas Taylor Sentenced for Broomstick Beating

Man sentenced for broomstick beating

Thomas E. Taylor was sentenced yesterday to two and one-half to five years in state prison for beating a man at a gambling parlor in 1982.

State Supreme Court Justice David O. Boehm approved a request by Taylor's lawyer, John F. Speranza Jr., that Taylor remain out of prison on more than $200,000 bail pending an appeal.

Taylor, 43, awaiting a second trial on murder charges in connection with the 1981 death of reputed mobster John N. Fiorino, was convicted July 6, 1983, for beating Samuel Alaimo with a broomstick. Thomas A. and Michael A. Pelusio also were convicted.

Alaimo said the three beat him with a broomstick, and punched and kicked him March 12, 1983, at the 44 Club, 44 Lake Ave.

The Pelusios had been sentenced Aug. 16, 1983, to two to six years in prison.

Aug. 4, 1984

While awaiting a second trial for the murder of John Fiorino, Thomas Taylor was finally sentenced for the March 12, 1982 beating of Samuel "Moe" Alaimo at the "44 Club."

Taylor had been convicted on July 6, 1983 of beating Alaimo with a broomstick, punching, and kicking him. His two co-defendants, Michael A. and Thomas A. Pelusio, had both been found guilty as well and were previously sentenced on Aug. 16 1983, to two to six years in prison.

Thomas Taylor was sentenced to two and one half to five years in state prison on **Aug. 3, 1984** for his part in the assault. State Supreme Court Justice David O. Boehm allowed Taylor to remain free on $200,000 bail that he had previously posted, pending an appeal. (62)

Torpey-Taylor Retrial Starts

Torpey-Taylor retrial starts today

The retrial of Thomas Torpey and Thomas Taylor for the Dec. 17, 1981 murder of John Fiorino began on **Jan. 22, 1985**. Immediately questions were raised about the possibility of finding a fair and impartial jury due to the notoriety of the defendants.

Thomas Taylor with attorney John Speranza at Taylor's first murder trial. Taylor had a new lawyer for his second trial, Robert Murphy.

The first trial lasted nearly four months and was the costliest trial in Monroe County history, costing the county $250,000. Jury selection in the trial took another eight weeks, due primarily to the near celebrity status of the defendants. It was very difficult to find a juror who had not heard of either Thomas Taylor or Thomas Torpey, or their well known association with organized crime.

Similar problems were expected for the second trial. If impartial jurors could not be found, the trial would have to be moved to another jurisdiction outside of Monroe County. A large part of the prosecution's case hinged on the testimony of Louis DiGuilio, who was serving a five to ten year sentence for conspiracy to commit murder. DiGuilio was also a member of the Federal Witness Protection Program. (63)

Thomas Torpey

Jury Selection Completed

Jury selection for the second trial was finally completed on **Feb. 14, 1985**. Opening statements were scheduled for **Feb. 19, 1985**. It took 15 days of questioning more than 500 potential jurors before a 12 person jury with four alternates was finally chosen. (64)

DiGiulio's Version of Fiorino Slaying Attacked

On **Feb. 22, 1985**, Louis DiGuilio was on the witness stand testifying to his version of events. DiGuilio, the getaway driver in the Fiorino murder, was allowed to plead guilty to a lesser charge of conspiracy to commit murder in exchange for testifying against his co-conspirators. He was sentenced to five to ten years in prison . He was eligible for parole in Dec. of 1986, less than two years away.

While cross-examining DiGuilio, Torpey's lawyer, David A. Murante painted a different picture of what took place on the night of the murder. According to Murante, the murder was DiGuilio's idea. DiGuilio, he said, was trying to gain favor with the established Mafia (A-Team) by killing Fiorino. Fiorino allegedly was helping Joe Rossi, Mafia Captain, and Rossi had been accused of stealing money from the crime family.

DiGuilio had been in a prison cell next to Rochester Mafia "Consigliore" Rene Piccarreto in Attica State Prison in 1977, while he (Rene) was temporarily incarcerated for the Massaro murder. DiGuilio claimed that he knew who Piccarreto was but he said they never talked about the Mafia. Under direct questioning, DiGuilio later admitted that he had aspired to become a "made" member of the Rochester Mafia.

"Did you have any aspiration to be a member of the Mob, a sworn member," Murante asked Diguilio.

"Yeah, the thought went through my mind," DiGuilio responded.

"How about December 1981, was that in your mind," Murante asked.

"Yeah, I guess it was," DiGuilio said.

"Were you aware that John Fiorino had a 'problem' with the crime family leadership," Murante asked DiGuilio.

"Whether he had a problem or not, I don't know. Look, all I know was he was helping Joe Rossi, and he wasn't supposed to be," Diguilio said.

"Did you know Fiorino was supposed to kill Rossi," Murante asked.

"That's what I heard," Diguilio said.

"Did you know he (Fiorino) was down and out with the mob," Murante asked.

"Yeah, I guess he was," said DiGuilio

"Why was Fiorino killed," asked Murante.

"He was the easiest guy to get," responded DiGuilio.

Near the end of his cross examination, Thomas Torpey's defense lawyer, David Murante, calmly walked over to where DiGuilio was seated in the witness chair and asked him a simple question.

"Why did the group, Taylor, Torpey, Sullivan and DiGuilio figure that the Mob would give up power if someone gunned down Fiorino, a member already in disfavor?"

"What do you mean how did we figure? We figured," exclaimed DiGuilio, slightly agitated, his voice rising for one of the few times during his entire testimony.

"How did you figure," Murante persisted.

"Why don't you ask your client," DiGuilio snapped back.

"I'm asking you, Mr. DiGuilio," Murante said.

"We all sat down and that's what came out, as simple as that, Fiorino's name came up by accident. You know it too! So why don't you knock it off," DiGuilio yelled at Murante.
(65)

Fiorino's Words on Fatal Night Recalled for Jury

The re-trial had started a little more than a year after the first trial ended in a mistrial. Closing arguments for the second murder trial were presented on **March 8, 1985**. The first trial had ended on Jan. 2, 1984 in a hung jury, and it was declared a mistrial.

During his summation of the new trial, Prosecutor Charles J. Siragusa asked the jury to remember Fiorino's last words to his wife before leaving his home.

"I'm going to the Blue Gardenia to meet the Eagle," Fiorino said to his wife as he left his house for the last time. Less than 30 minutes later, John Fiorino, Mafia Captain, was laying dead in the parking lot of the Blue Gardenia.

Siragusa then pointed at Thomas Taylor and said, "That, ladies and gentlemen, is The Eagle."

At another point during his closing arguments, which lasted for more than one hour, Siragusa was equally dramatic. With an outstretched arm he pointed towards Torpey and Taylor and told the jury that they were,

"**Nothing more and nothing less than cold-blooded murderers. Calculated and callous. Together with DiGuilio and Sullivan they planned and effected the execution of John Fiorino."** (42)

Jury Deliberations

The trial was over. Prosecutor Charles J. Siragusa had presented almost 40 witnesses in the second trial. But the case hinged on the testimony of one of those witnesses, Louis DiGuilio, an admitted participant in the plot, who turned informant.

Jury deliberations began on **March 11, 1985**, at about 11:30 a.m. The jury deliberated for nearly seven hours without reaching a verdict. Deliberations resumed the following day, **March 12, 1985**, at 9 a.m. (66)

Before the day was over the jury reached a verdict, **Guilty!** In the first trial, the jury had deliberated for six days and still could not reach a verdict. This time was different.

Torpey reacted angrily and began yelling at the prosecutor, Charles J. Siragusa, before he was dragged out of the courtroom by sheriff's deputies. Thomas Taylor, who had been free on $200,000 bail, was quietly taken into custody. (67)

Taylor later stated, "This is a case for the "Birds." DiGiulio was a "Stool Pigeon," Taylor is the "Eagle," and Siragusa's nickname was the "Goose."

Judge Gives Torpey-Taylor the Maximum

On **March 12, 1985**, Thomas Taylor had remained silent after being found guilty of murder by a jury of his peers. But nearly a month later, on **April 9, 1985**, as Taylor was being sentenced, he became argumentative with the judge. Both Torpey and Taylor continued to profess their innocence before Judge Kennedy, but to no avail.

In a stinging rebuke, state Supreme Court Justice Robert P. Kennedy looked at Torpey and said, **"You certainly don't have to answer to me, but you sure answered to the jury! And now, especially, you answer to the law. As much as you'd like to be, you are not above the law!"**

Then later, Judge Kennedy's temper flared up again. This time his anger was directed toward Thomas Taylor after Taylor had interrupted him.

"That's enough! That's enough! Stop your talking. I've listened to you long enough," Judge Kennedy yelled back at Taylor.

"You apparently feel Mr. Taylor, you're the king," Kennedy continued.

"No, you do your honor," Taylor responded.

"But I understand you don't have the guts to do your own dirty work," Judge Kennedy snapped back, referring to the fact that Torpey and Taylor had hired another person, Joseph Sullivan, to kill Fiorino.

At first Thomas Torpey was silent as he stood before Judge Kennedy awaiting sentencing, and then in a taunting fashion Judge Kennedy held up a copy of a March 18, 1985 Times Union newspaper article in which Torpey stated, during an interview, that he did not have to answer to either the judge or the jury for his conduct. It seemed to be a deliberate attempt by the judge to agitate Torpey.

Torpey quickly interrupted Judge Kennedy, declaring, **"Except to God your honor. We all answer to God your honor. I'll be alright when that day comes."**

During that interview with the Times Union newspaper, Torpey stated that he expected Judge Kennedy to impose the maximum sentence sought by the prosecutor, Charles J. Siragusa.

"I don't want to disappoint you," Judge Kennedy said to Thomas Torpey before sentencing him to 25 years to life in prison. (68)

Torpey and Taylor Sentenced To 25 to Life For the Murder of John Fiorino

Thomas Torpey

Thomas Taylor

On **April 9, 1985**, Thomas Torpey and Thomas Taylor, Rochester Mafia "C Team" leaders, were both sentenced to 25 years to life for ordering the murder of Rochester Mafia "Captain" John Fiorino of the "A Team," on Dec. 17, 1981.

John was Vice-President of Teamsters Local #398 at the time of his death. Thomas Torpey and Thomas Taylor were both former bodyguards for the late Sammy Gingello, Rochester Mafia "Underboss." (43)

Torpey, Taylor given 25-year-to-life terms

Chapter 10
Dominick Taddeo
- Hitman-

Oct. 8, 1987 Democrat and Chronicle

Hitman Named in 3 Killings Ordered by Former Mob Chief

Rene Piccarreto ordered killings.

Reputed mobster Dominic Taddeo committed three gangland slayings in the early 1980's under the orders of former mob leader Rene Piccarreto. Taddeo killed Nicholas Mastrodonato, Gerald Pelusio, and Dino Tortatice in revenge for the murder of mob leader John Fiorino, and to eliminate an insurgent faction of the Mafia called the "C-Team," said Rochester Police Investigator Paul Camping.

Camping submitted an 11 page affidavit on **Oct. 7, 1987** at hearings that were being held to determine whether bail should be set for reputed mobsters Loren Piccarreto, Angelo Amico, and Joseph LoDolce, who were indicted the previous week on extortion, racketeering, and conspiracy charges.

Camping also claimed that local mob leaders were upset due to all the publicity surrounding the indictments causing some local bookmakers to discontinue making extortion payments to the Mob. A reputed Mafia member was also quoted in the affidavit as saying, **"We are going to have to make 'examples' of some of the bookmakers."** (44)

(Dominic Taddeo's Mob Hits)
Dominic Taddeo is Indicted for Slaying 3 Mobsters

Dominic Taddeo of Rochester, N.Y., described by authorities as an organized crime figure, was indicted on **Aug. 1, 1990**, on two racketeering counts that linked him to three homicides and two attempted homicides in the Rochester area, U.S. Attorney Dennis C. Vacco said.

At the time, Taddeo, 33, was already in prison. He had been implicated in **July of 1990** in a plot to use guns and camouflage gear stored in rented lockers in the Lehigh Valley to bust Colombian cocaine lord Carlos Lehder out of federal prison, and sell him back to the Medellin Drug Cartel. Taddeo randomly chose the Lehigh Valley, officials said.

That plan was interrupted with Taddeo's March 1989 arrest in Cleveland and the subsequent seizure of the weapons and cash stored in lockers in Bethlehem and Wescosville, police said. Taddeo was serving a 17-year federal sentence for possession of illegal weapons and bail jumping.

Aug. 2, 1990
Democrat and Chronicle

The federal grand jury indicted Taddeo under the Racketeer Influenced Corrupt Organizations Act. Evidence presented to the grand jury by Assistant U.S. Attorneys Christopher Buscaglia and Anthony Bruce was developed over a three and a half year investigation.

Count one of the indictment alleged that Taddeo was part of the Rochester La Cosa Nostra Crime Family, participated in the May 25, 1982 murder of Nicholas Mastrodonato; the Aug. 27, 1982 murder of Gerald Pelusio; the April 12 and Nov. 10, 1983 attempted murders of Thomas Marotta; the Aug. 2, 1983 murder of Dino Tortatice; and a conspiracy to murder Thomas Taylor, Vacco said.

It also alleged that Taddeo conducted an illegal gambling business in Rochester and used extortion to take over another gambling business, then ran a gambling operation from that business. Count two charged Taddeo with conspiring to conduct affairs named in the first count. Each count of the indictment carried a maximum penalty of 20 years in prison and a $250,000 fine. (45)

Taddeo Pleads Guilty In Mob Hits

On Saturday, **Jan. 25, 1992**, nearly a decade after the last of the so-called .45-caliber slayings rocked the Rochester underworld, suspected hit man Dominic Taddeo finally appeared before a federal judge and said five significant words,

"Guilty. Guilty. Guilty. Guilty. Guilty."

It was a surprise unannounced development in the long-standing case that was scheduled to go to trial in March of 1992. The 34-year-old former Greece man admitted that he had plotted five Mafia killings and succeeded in carrying out three of them.

Dominic Taddeo

Taddeo pleaded guilty to both counts of a two-count indictment charging him with racketeering for the 1981 and 1982 slayings and for operating illegal gambling establishments in Rochester. He also pleaded guilty on three weapons counts.

Appearing before U.S. District Judge Michael A. Telesca, Taddeo was asked if facts outlined by the prosecutor were true:

1) That, a crime organization known as La Cosa Nostra existed in Rochester in 1982.

"Yes," said Taddeo.

2) That he was paid by the organization to kill certain people.

"Yes," said Taddeo.

3) That he conducted surveillance of intended targets and executed several crimes.

"Yes," said Taddeo.

Victims of the so-called "45-caliber slayings" described in that indictment were Nicholas Mastrodonato, shot to death May 25, 1982; Gerald Pelusio, shot Aug. 27, 1982; and Dino Tortatice, killed Aug. 2, 1983. Taddeo also was accused of shooting mob leader Thomas Marotta twice in 1981 in failed attempts to kill him, and plotting to kill Thomas Taylor and Bobby Comfort, C-Team Mob figures.

The shootings had taken place during a period that produced considerable violence among rival factions of the local mob. Rochester Police Department Investigator Paul Camping, part of a strike force set up to monitor organized crime activity in Monroe County, said, "I've been tracking this guy (Taddeo) since 1976." (46)

On **April 16, 1992**, Dominic Taddeo was sentenced to 20 years in prison for committing three murders. He received four extra years for weapons possession, for a total of 24 years. The sentence was ordered to run consecutively with the 30 year sentence previously inflicted on him for bail jumping, weapons possession, and drug charges. Taddeo must serve at least 30 years before he is eligible for parole.

Prior to sentencing, in scathing oratory, Judge Michael A. Telesca looked at Taddeo and said,

"You have not shown any remorse for any of your criminal activity, including the taking of three lives."

Dominic Taddeo, left, is escorted from the courtroom by a police officer.

But despite the harsh words, the sentence was rather light for three murders. Telesca noted at the time that he could have sentenced Taddeo to up to 70 years, but he took into consideration defense lawyer Culver Barr's statement that the guilty pleas eliminated the need for costly trials! (52)

Dominic Taddeo is currently incarcerated at Coleman Medium FCI and is scheduled for release on March 29, 2023.

Conclusion

Tom Torpey and I were tried twice. The first trial ended in a hung jury, 9-3 for conviction, after four months of trial from 9-5 each day plus six days of juror deliberations. John Speranza represented me, and Felix Lapine represented Torpey. They both did a fine job, considering all that they had to overcome.

The second trial was different. We had different lawyers. There was a different Judge and a different District Attorney. The second trial lasted only six weeks, with three days of juror deliberations. The verdict was Guilty!

For this trial we had Judge Kennedy, who was known as the "Hanging Judge." Judge Kennedy still lived with his mother in the house where he was born. He had never married and he never had any children. Judge Kennedy went to Mass and took communion every day. He was not stamping out crime, he was stamping out sin.

Tom Torpey and I were both sentenced to 25 years to life and we both had other indictments and convictions pending, which had yet to be attended to. Who knew what the future held. I was going through a divorce with my wife and had a wonderful relationship with a young lady named Nancy Acker.

I told her on one of her prison visits that our relationship had to change since she was a young, beautiful woman with her whole life ahead of her and I might never get out (of prison)! Of course she was upset and pledged her love. She swore she would never marry unless it was to me. She never did marry and in 2009 I was paroled. In 2010 we were married.

After serving a full 25 years, Thomas Taylor was released from prison in 2009. Shortly thereafter, on April 3, 2010, Tom Taylor and Nancy Acker were married (left).

Making Parole

My oldest daughter, Laura, played a crucial role in my parole. She has been my guiding light for 25 years for family support and emotional support. She has five beautiful children three girls and two boys.

She was there to pick me up in 2009 when I was released on parole. I never made parole before on two other sentences. Three times previously I had been before the parole board and three times I was shot down. So how was I going to overcome my record this time? Violence, organized crime and two more convictions with the 44 Club assault and the Federal case.

Thomas Taylor and his daughter Laura crammed together in a photo booth at Wende Correctional Facility around the year 2000.

Judges normally write Parole Boards and say such and such inmate should not be paroled for whatever reason. Why not have a judge write the Parole Board and recommend certain inmates for parole? So my attorney, John Speranza, spoke to Judge Mark, who wrote to the Parole Board on my behalf. Judge Mark presided over my first murder trial, which ended in a mistrial.

Pastor Vince DiPaola of Lakeshore Community Church in Greece, N.Y. also wrote a wonderful letter to the Parole Board for me. They have a Violence and Substance Abuse Recovery Program run by Andy Britt, a friend of mine, and childhood friend Phillip Argento, who sponsored me.

I was never a very religious man, but after being blown up in the car and living, with only the armrest between Sammy and I and Sammy laying on the ground, a cloud of smoke over me, it was like being blown into the Kingdom of God, because it was certainly "divine intervention" that I survived. I should have accepted it then instead of continuing on with my way of life.

So here I was, going to the Parole Board after that way of life had me imprisoned for 25 years. Even with the letters, the chances of making parole were not good. But to my surprise, and against all odds, I was paroled.

It was "divine intervention" again. This time I accepted it changing my way of life. Upon release I went to church that Sunday and thanked Pastor Vince DiPaolo for taking a chance on me with his letter. I also thanked Judge Mark and Attorney Speranza. I was released on Aug. 9th, 2009 and lived with my son, Mark Silveri, who incidentally and coincidently is nephew to Bobby Silveri.

I am catching up on lost time with my children and grandchildren and on April 3, 2010, I married Nancy Acker. We've been happily married ever since.

Hon. Donald J. Mark
Supreme Court Justice (RET)
545 Hall of Justice
Rochester, New York 14614

March 27, 2009

State of New York
Executive Department
Division of Parole
97 Central Avenue
Albany, New York 12206

Attention: Mr. Lester G. Edwards

Re: Thomas E. Taylor

Dear Mr. Edwards:

    This letter is written on behalf of Thomas E. Taylor, presently incarcerated at the Wende Correctional Facility and eligible to be released on parole.

    I was the County Court Judge who presided over his first trial, which after four months of trial and seven days of deliberation, a mistrial was declared, because in this circumstantial case the jury was split 9 to 3 for conviction.

    There were three contacts between me and Mr. Taylor which created a favorable impression.

    While he was out on bail before his second trial concluded we met accidentally at a restaurant, and he, knowing that as a Marine veteran I collected Marine memorabilia, promised me something for my collection. While serving his sentence after his conviction he arranged for a deliver of a historical book to my chambers.

    In the flap of the book he had written "To Judge Donald Mark, a fair judge". I was pleased with that characterization because many rulings during the trial were adverse to the defense.

    There was an insert in the book in which he had written in essence that he had joined the Marines at age 16, that his father had intercepted him in Buffalo

Page one of the letter Judge Donald J. Mark wrote to the Parole Board on behalf of Thomas Taylor.

(where recruits from this area leave for boot camp) and that without this intervention history would have been different.

Based upon the reputation that preceded Mr. Taylor at his trial, his institutional record was a pleasant surprise.

He had one minor infraction of the facility's rules from 1985 to 2009, and in his inmate program report dated 4/28/96, he was marked three "excellents", six "above averages" and two "average"; in his inmate program report dated 2/23/05 his eleven markings were all "above average"; and his inmate program report dated 1/20/09 his eleven markings were all "above average". He also successfully completed a food service certificate program on 3/22/02, and he received a high mark in that area on 1/20/09.

Mr. Taylor in his ASAT evaluation scored 18 points which was "above average", successfully completed the six months competency based ASAT program and passed his mental hygiene examination.

He is almost 70 years old and not in the best of physical health, has strong family ties, has made satisfactory living arrangements and has offers of employment, all of which are indicative of a crime free post-incarceration life. This conclusion is reinforced by his history of adjustment, his work record, his compliance with the facility and rules and his positive participation in its programs.

An interesting facet of this case is that Mr. Taylor has served 25 years in a correctional facility for a murder committed by a co-defendant although under the law because of Section 20.00 of the Penal law he was equally guilty.

It is my recommendation that Thomas E. Taylor be released on parole as soon as he becomes eligible for the same.

Thank you for your consideration in this matter.

Very truly yours,

Donald J. Mark
Supreme Court Justice (RET)

DJM:rw

Page two of the letter Judge Donald J. Mark wrote to the Parole Board on behalf of Thomas Taylor.

FOOTNOTES

1) Dec. 18. 1981 Democrat and Chronicle "Mob Figure shot dead"
2) Democrat and Chronicle Rochester, New York
 Dec. 19, 1981, Sat • Page 1 "Mafia War Feared," Democrat and Chronicle Rochester, New York Dec. 18, 1981, Sat • Page 1 "Mob figure slain in Irondequoit"
3) Democrat and Chronicle Rochester, New York Dec. 18, 1981, Fri • Page 3 "Victim was Informant"

4) Democrat and Chronicle Rochester, New York 19 Dec 1981, Sat • Page 1 "Mafia War Feared"
5) Daily News New York, New York 24 Feb 1982, Wed • Page 3 "Mad dog Killer Who Fled Attica in 71 is Caught" ;Feb. 24, 1982 Democrat & Chronicle Pic of Denonville Hotel
6) The Record Hackensack, New Jersey 25 Feb 1982, Thu • Page 19 "Prosecutor Wants to See Mad Dog"
7) Democrat and Chronicle Rochester, New York 27 Feb 1982, Sat • Page 6 "Sullivan Arraigned on Robbery Charges"
8) Democrat and Chronicle Rochester, New York
16 Mar 1982, Tue • Page 7 "Children find Shotgun Believed Used in Slaying"
9) Democrat and Chronicle Rochester, New York
26 Mar 1982, Fri • Page 5 "Mad Dog Sullivan Denies 2 Slaying Charges in Suffolk County"
10) May 26, 1982 Democrat and Chronicle "Man Linked to Local Mob Shot to Death in Coin Store"
11) Democrat and Chronicle Rochester, New York, 08 Jun 1982, Tue • Page 9 "Testimony to Start in DiGuilio Trial"
12) June 9, 1982 Democrat and Chronicle "DiGiulio Ends His Silence Torpey and Taylor Arrested"
13) Democrat and Chronicle Rochester, New York 09 Jun 1982, Wed • Page 3 'Thomas Taylor has 4 convictions for assault, served 8 years for Extortion"
14) Democrat and Chronicle Rochester, New York
02 Jul 1982, Fri • Page 3 "$500,000 Bail for Taylor";Democrat and Chronicle Rochester, New York
16 Jun 1982, Wed • Page 15 "Bail Decision Reserved on Thomas Taylor"

FOOTNOTES

15) Daily News , New York, New York
26 Jun 1982, Sat • Page 82 "Mad Dog Sullivan Acquitted in Heist"
16) Democrat and Chronicle, Rochester, New York
13 Aug 1982, Fri • Page 7 "Cursing Sullivan is Hauled from Court After Judge Denies His Request"
17) Democrat and Chronicle, Rochester, New York
18 Aug 1982, Wed • Page 6 "Sullivan: I'm No Hit Man"
18) Democrat and Chronicle, Rochester, New York
29 Aug 1982, Sun • Page 2 "Case of Mistaken Identity"
19) Democrat and Chronicle, Rochester, New York
28 Aug 1982, Sat • Page 2 Gangland Retaliation Feared"
20) Sep. 4, 1982 Democrat and Chronicle "Pelusio Leads Mob Faction"
21) Democrat and Chronicle, Rochester, New York
10 Sep 1982, Fri • Page 3 "Joseph Sullivan Trial Opens"
22) Democrat and Chronicle, Rochester, New York
11 Sep 1982, Sat • Page 4 "Sullivan's Girlfriend Fails to Show"
23) Democrat and Chronicle, Rochester, New York
15 Sep 1982, Wed • Page 2 "DiGuilio Tells Court of Stalking Victims"
24) September 16, 1982 Democrat & Chronicle "Sullivan Berates Prosecutor"
25) Democrat and Chronicle Rochester, New York
21 Sep 1982, Tue • Page "Sullivan Case Rests Without Him Being Called to Testify"
26) Democrat and Chronicle Rochester, New York
24 Sep 1982, Fri • Page 4 "Sullivan Found Guilty in Slaying of Fiorino"
27) Daily News New York, New York
08 Oct 1982, Fri • Page 134 "Mad dog Sullivan Draws 25-to-life for murder rap"
28) Democrat and Chronicle Rochester, New York
14 Oct 1982, Thu • Page 17 "Eyeball Treatment"
29) October 20, 1982   Democrat and Chronicle "Three Mob Figures Indicted on Weapons Charges"
30) Daily News New York, New York
25 Nov 1982, Thu • Page 110 "Mad dog Sullivan Guilty"
31) April 13, 1983 Democrat and Chronicle "Marotta Says He Didn't See Assailant"
32) August 4, 1983 Democrat and Chronicle "Slain Gang Leader's Ambition May Have Led Mob to Order His Death"

FOOTNOTES

33) Nov. 11, 1983 Democrat and Chronicle"Marotta Gunned Down Again"

34) Democrat and Chronicle November 12, 1983 "Friends of Slain Gang Leader Arrested in Area After Marotta **Shooting**"

35) Democrat and Chronicle Rochester, New York
16 Nov 1983, Wed • Page 6 "Policeman tells of his close call on Night Fiorino Slain"; http://www.fivefamiliesnyc.com/2017/06/notorious-rochester-hit-man-dies-in.html

36) Democrat and Chronicle Rochester, New York
17 Nov 1983, Thu • Page 5 "Informant Tells of Bitterness Between Torpey and Rochester Mob"

37) Democrat and Chronicle Rochester, New York
18 Nov 1983, Fri • Page 2 "You Put the Finger of Death on Fiorino, Defense Lawyer Tells Witness"

38) Democrat and Chronicle Rochester, New York
27 Nov 1983, Sun • Page 4 "The Gospel according to Louie"

39) December 2, 1983 Democrat and Chronicle "Lawyer Claims Judge Blocked Sullivan From Clearing Torpey"

40) December 9, 1983 Democrat and Chronicle "Fiorino's Widow on Stand, Recalls Last Hour She Spent With Husband"

41) Democrat and Chronicle Rochester, New York
25 Dec 1983, Sun • Page 29 "Mob Trials pic of Torpey, Taylor and Sullivan"

42) Democrat and Chronicle Rochester, New York
09 Mar 1985, Sat • Page 4 "Fiorino's Words on Fatal Night Recalled"

43) April 10, 1985 Democrat & Chronicle "Torpey and Taylor Sentenced to 25 to Life For the Murder of John Fiorino"

44) October 8, 1987 Democrat and Chronicle "Hitman Named in 3 Killings"

45) August 2, 1990 Democrat and Chronicle "Dominic Taddeo is Indicted in Three Slayings"

46) Saturday, January 25, 1992, Democrat and Chronicle "Taddeo Pleads Guilty in Mob Hits"

47) Press and Sun-Bulletin Binghamton, New York
19 May 1971, Wed • Page 7 "Escapee Not Telling How"

48) Star-Gazette (Elmira, New York)
20 May 1943, Thu • Page 25 "LaPlaca Faces Life Sentence"

49) Democrat and Chronicle, Rochester, New York
13 May 2018, Sun • Page A19 "Picture of Malsegna"

50) Democrat and Chronicle, Rochester, New York
23 Oct 1970, Fri • Page 11 Pic of Charles Russo"

FOOTNOTES

51) Democrat and Chronicle Rochester, New York
13 May 2018, Sun • Page A1 "Where Were Cops when Sammy G Died?" Picture of inside of car
52) Democrat and Chronicle Rochester, New York
16 Apr 1992, Thu • Page 5 "Taddeo Gets 24 Years in an Angry Judgement"
53) Democrat and Chronicle Rochester, New York
20 Mar 1982, Sat • Page 14 "Taylor and Marino Indicted"
54) Democrat and Chronicle Rochester, New York
02 Jul 1982, Fri • Page 3 "$500,000 Bail for Taylor"
55) Democrat and Chronicle Rochester, New York
14 Mar 1982, Sun • Page 29 "Grand Jury to Hear of Assault"
56) Democrat and Chronicle Rochester, New York
15 Mar 1982, Mon • Page 7 "Police Confiscate Mob Figure's Car": Democrat and Chronicle Rochester, New York
17 Mar 1982, Wed • Page 4 "No Charges Filed"
57) Democrat and Chronicle Rochester, New York
23 Mar 1982, Tue • Page 5 "Social Club With Links to Mob Hit by Fire of Unknown Cause"
58) Democrat and Chronicle Rochester, New York
01 Jul 1983, Fri • Page 39 "Three Men Give Conflicting Testimony in Taylor Pelusio assault Case"
59) Democrat and Chronicle Rochester, New York
06 Jul 1983, Wed • Page 16 "Assault Trial of 3 Reputed Mobsters Going to Jury Today"
60) Democrat and Chronicle Rochester, New York
07 Jul 1983, Thu • Page 9 "Guilty Verdicts for Pelusio and Taylor"
61) Democrat and Chronicle Rochester, New York
17 Aug 1983, Wed • Page 14 "2 Receive 2 to 6 Year Terms for Assault Convictions";Democrat and Chronicle Rochester, New York
04 Aug 1984, Sat • Page 11 " Man sentenced for Broomstick Beating"
62) Democrat and Chronicle Rochester, New York
04 Aug 1984, Sat • Page 11 "Man Sentenced for Broomstick Beating"
63) Democrat and Chronicle Rochester, New York
22 Jan 1985, Tue • Page 8 "Torpey-Taylor Retrial Starts Today"
64) Democrat and Chronicle Rochester, New York
15 Feb 1985, Fri • Page 11 "Jury Selection Completed"

FOOTNOTES

65) Democrat and Chronicle Rochester, New York
23 Feb 1985, Sat • Page 15 DiGiulio's Version of Fiorino Slaying Attacked"
66) Democrat and Chronicle Rochester, New York
12 Mar 1985, Tue • Page 12 "Torpey-Taylor Jury Continues Deliberations"
67) Democrat and Chronicle Rochester, New York
13 Mar 1985, Wed • Page 1 "Lawyers Credit Streamlined Trial for Convictions of Torpey, Taylor"
68) Democrat and Chronicle Rochester, New York
10 Apr 1985, Wed • Page 6 "Judge Gives Torpey-Taylor the Maximum"
69) Democrat and Chronicle Rochester, New York
21 Dec 1983, Wed • Page 20 "Perjurers Being Put on Stand Prosecutor Says"
70) "Mad Dog' Sullivan Arraigned in Syracuse in 1982
Updated Feb 24, 2017; Posted Feb 24, 2017 By Johnathan Croyle jcroyle@syracuse.com, syracuse.com
71) Democrat and Chronicle Rochester, New York
24 Apr 1983, Sun • Page 8 "Marotta Probe Focuses on 8 Young Eastsiders"Democrat and Chronicle Rochester, New York
21 Apr 1983, Thu • Page 7 "Several Questioned in Shooting"; Democrat and Chronicle Rochester, New York
30 Jul 1982, Fri • Page 6 "Charged With Assaults"
72) Democrat and Chronicle Rochester, New York
07 Jun 1950, Wed • Page 1 "Terra Brothers Found Guilty of Weapon count"
73) Picture on Facebook by Ben Borrelli
74) Democrat and Chronicle Rochester, New York
07 Feb 1982, Sun • Page 21 "Club Fire Believed an accident"
75) Democrat and Chronicle Rochester, New York
27 May 1970, Wed • Page 20 "A 23 year old Man Arrested"; Democrat and Chronicle Rochester, New York
20 Aug 1964, Thu • Page 21 "Three Placed on Probation as Youthful Offenders"; Democrat and Chronicle Rochester, New York
19 Apr 1970, Sun • Page 43 "Man Found Guilty in Narcotics Case."

Dominick "The Deacon" Allocco was a gambler who was murdered Feb. 23, 1965. Allocco was a messenger boy for Rochester Mob Boss Jake Russo. One evening, while delivering a message to Norman Huck, Huck knocked him out while saying "I won't be able to make the meeting but give this to Jake Russo for me," as he slugged him.

William "Billy" Barton was a career criminal and longtime friend of Thomas Taylor. Taylor and Barton committed many crimes together starting as far back as the early 1960's. Barton and Taylor had a falling out and Barton joined the "B-Team" supporting Thomas DiDio in the Mob war. Barton mistakenly thought the A-Team leaders would never get out of jail.

Johnny "Broadway" Cavagrotti was a gambler. He owned the Goodman Novelty Shop, which was a front for a gambling operation. John J. "Broadway" Cavagrotti disappeared on Sept. 21, 1967 and was presumed dead. He was last seen getting into a car with Sammy Gingello, who was a suspect in the disappearance, although he was never charged.

Dominic "Sonny" Celestino was once beat up and kicked out of the Rochester Mafia Family in 1975, on the orders of Sammy Gingello for violating one of the rules of the Organization, He returned in 1977 when Gingello, Piccaretto, and Russotti were put in jail. He then became the leader of the "B Team" after Thomas Didio was murdered in 1978. He was directly responsible for killing "Sammy G."

Dominic Chirico was a Rochester Mafia Captain, during the Valenti era. He was murdered in 1972 to send a message to Frank Valenti to step down as Boss of the Rochester Mafia. His murder was the real beginning of "The Rochester Mob Wars."

Robert "Bobby" Comfort was a notorious career criminal gaining fame for masterminding the 1972 Hotel Pierre Robbery in New York City. He was friends with Thomas Taylor and was a C-Team member along with his brother, Paul. He was standing right next to Gerald Pelusio when he (Pelusio) was murdered.

Eugene DiFrancesco was a Soldier in the Rochester Mafia. He was also the triggerman in the Jimmy "The Hammer" Massaro murder. He was imprisoned, released and put back in prison for that murder.

Lucien DiGiovanni was a Vice-Squad Detective. But he was a crooked cop who was protecting Numbers Banker Abe Hamza. DiGiovanni was caught by FBI surveillance having a secret meeting with Rochester Mafia Boss Frank Valenti. The revelation of that meeting led to several investigations and disciplinary action.

Louis DiGiulio was the getaway driver for Joseph Sullivan. He was a participant of the murder of John Fiorino. Diguilio turned "state's evidence" and testified against his co-conspirators in exchange for a lighter sentence. He then entered into the Federal Witness Protection Program.

John Fiorino was a Rochester Mafia Captain. He was murdered outside of the Blue Gardenia restaurant on Dec. 17, 1981 by Joseph Sullivan. Thomas Torpey and Thomas Taylor were tried, convicted, and sentenced to 25 years to life for hiring Sullivan to commit the murder.

Salvatore "Sammy G" Gingello was the "Underboss" of the Rochester Mafia until he was murdered on April 23, 1978 by a car bomb. Thomas Taylor, Sam's bodyguard/driver was sitting in the front passenger seat at the time of the explosion.

Abe Hamza, the Numbers Banker, was protected by Lucian DiGiovanni, who was a Rochester Police Department Vice-Squad Detective Sargeant.

Norman Huck was good friends with Thomas Taylor and Al Mancuso. He also became good friends with Charles "Chip the Wolf" LaPlaca while in prison. Huck once had a confrontation with Rochester Mafia Boss Jake Russo that ended with Huck pouring a bottle of champagne over Russo's head. He was murdered in 1965.

Charles "Chip The Wolf" LaPlaca was a notorious gangster sentenced to 65 years for murder. He became friends with Norman Huck in Prison. He was at one time friends with Rochester Mafia Boss Jake Russo, but the two had a falling out.

William "Billy" Lupo (Rochester Mafia Capo) was shot to death in April of 1970 for allegedly stealing $100,000 from Sammy G's house. The two were next door neighbors. Lupo was allegedly business partners with Chief of Detectives William Mahoney in illegal gambling ventures.

Liam Magee was in Attica prison with Thomas Taylor and Joe Sullivan. Liam helped Sullivan escape from prison in 1971. He remained friends with Joe and years later Liam brought some money to Joe at motel he was staying at. Liam was an Irish Folk Singer who played regularly in the Rochester area. He was also a C-Team member.

William "Back Room Bill" Mahoney was Chief of Detectives. He was accused of obtaining confessions by beating them out of the suspects. Several of his convictions were overturned for this reason. He also was alleged to have been providing protection for Billy Lupo's gambling joint and sharing in the profits.

Anthony Malsegna was a Monroe County Sherriff's Deputy. He was one of several police officers, recruited by Bill Mahoney, who fabricated evidence and falsely testified at the Massaro murder trials in order to convict the top echelon of the Rochester Mafia in 1977.

Al Mancuso was a career criminal. He was indicted for the murder of Ben Oken but was acquitted of that charge. He was arrested with Thomas Taylor and Ben Morganti for attempted extortion of a numbers banker. All three men were sentenced to lengthy prison terms in Attica State Prison.

Tom Marotta was a Rochester Mafia Captain. He was imprisoned in 1984 on murder and conspiracy charges along with the rest of the hierarch of the A-Team faction of the Rochester Mob. He resumed his criminal activity after his release and plead guilty to several felonies in 2002 plea agreement, naming all his co-conspirators.

Vincent "Jimmy The Hammer" Massaro was murdered in 1973 on the orders of the Rochester Mafia hierarchy. Before his demise, Massaro had worked with Norman Huck and Tom Taylor on various jobs. Massaro was also a hit-man and arsonist for the Rochester Mafia. He was one of two likely suspects in Norman Huck's murder.

Rene Piccarreto Rochester Mafia "Consigliore" ordered the murder of all C-Team members involved in John Fiorino's murder. He paid Dominic Taddeo $500 for each murder. Piccarreto also ordered the murder of Mafia Captain Thomas Marotta, allegedly for cooperating with the police. Marotta was shot twice but survived both times.

Thomas Pelusio was the front man of the C-Team following the arrest of Taylor and Torpey on murder charges. Pelusio's brother Gerald was murdered by the "A-Team" in a case of mistaken identity. The intended target of course was Thomas, who looked very much like his brother Gerald. Pelusio entered the Witness Protection Program.

Sam Rangatore, Buffalo Mob "Soldier," was in Rochester being surveilled by the FBI. That surveillance led to the discovery of a secret meeting taking place at a joint on State Street between Vice Squad Detective Lucian DiGiovanni and Rochester Mafia Boss Frank Valenti.

Joe "The Hop" Rossi was the Mafia "Captain." Thomas Taylor worked for him when the A and B Wars were taking place. Joe approved the recruitment of Joseph Sullivan in an unfulfilled plan to eliminate members of the B-Team.

Charlie Russo was Jake Russo's brother. Charlie was involved in a scheme to defraud "Sammy G" in a dice game using loaded dice. When the scheme was discovered, Charlie suffered a severe beating for his "disrespect" of Sammy Gingello.

Jake Russo was the "Boss" of the Rochester Mafia in the early 1960's. Benny Morganti allegedly got Jake's permission to shake down Abe Hamza. Jake was murdered in October of 1964.

Samuel "Red" Russotti was the Boss of the Rochester Mafia in the early 1970's and 1980's. He was also Joey Tiraborelli's step-father.

Joseph Sullivan was the first and only man to escape from Attica State Prison, on April 9, 1971, by hiding under sacks of flour on a delivery truck.

Dominic Taddeo was a hit-man hired by Rene Piccarreto, "Consigliore" of the Rochester Mafia, to murder all C-Team faction members that had anything to do with the murder of John Fiorino. Taddeo was credited with three murders and at least two attempted murders committed on the orders of the A-Team.

Thomas Taylor, Rochester Mob Associate was first imprisoned in 1964 for extortion. He later became Sammy G's bodyguard and driver until Sam's death. Taylor then had a falling out with the established Mob and hired Mad Dog Sullivan to Kill Mob Captain John Fiorino. Taylor served 25 years and was released in 2009.

Joey Tiraborelli was the step-son of Rochester Mafia "Boss" Samuel Russotti. Joey once whacked Thomas Taylor on the side of the head giving him a dozen stitches before Taylor pistol whipped him, giving Joey twice as many stiches. He also once tried to have Taylor "taken for a ride."

Thomas Torpey was Sammy G's bodyguard. He was in the car when Sammy died. Torpey was battling the established Mafia at the same time Taylor was. He was refusing to pay his "vig" money to the A-Team on his Lyell Avenue gambling joint. Together they formed the "C-Team."

Joe "Lead-Pipe Joe" Todaro Jr. was a Buffalo Mafia Boss. Rochester Mobsters were subservient to the Buffalo Organization and often had to seek permission to do things. Thomas Taylor once attended a meeting in Florida where the Rochester Bosses met Todaro seeking permission for a business venture there.

Dino Tortatice was mistakenly accused of being a member of the C-Team, an insurgent faction of mobsters warring with the established Mob (A-Team). He had a personal beef with Joey Tiraborelli for mistreating his sister. He was murdered outside of his mother's home on Aug. 2, 1983.

Appendix

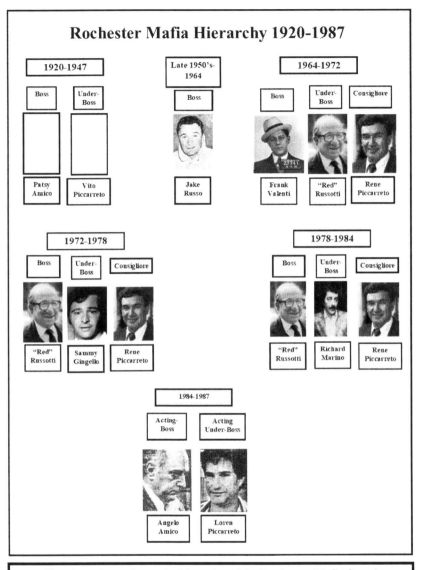

The chart above shows the hierarchy of the Rochester Mafia from its pre-prohibition beginning until its demise in the late 1980's. Patsy Amico ruled the crime family until his death in 1947. For the next ten years the leadership of the family was obscure. Both Frank and Stanley Valenti attended the infamous Nov. 14, 1957 Appalachin Summit and were jailed. Jake Russo was left in charge until his 1964 murder, when Frank Valenti regained control. Valenti was overthrown in 1972 and the new leaders were jailed in 1984, causing temporary leaders to be appointed before their own imprisonment in 1987. By then, the Rochester Family was only a shell of its original size.

Appendix

Liam Magee

Liam Magee, performing in Rochester, N.Y. in 1995.

Liam Magee was a native of Ireland, who grew up on 189 Lexington Ave. in Rochester, N.Y. In 1964, when he was 17 years old, he was convicted of burglary charges for breaking into Nazareth Academy, a Catholic School on Lake Avenue. He was given a suspended, Elmira Reception Center sentence and placed on three years probation.

Six years later, when he was 23 years old, he was convicted of first degree possession of a dangerous drug. He was caught with three pounds of marijuana at the Rochester-Monroe County Airport. Another seven pounds had been removed from a package sent to Magee by California Bureau of Narcotics agents before the package left San Diego. He was sentenced to five years and sent to Attica State Prison in 1970.

While in prison, Liam became friends with both Thomas Taylor and Joseph Sullivan. Taylor was serving time for extortion and Sullivan was serving time for a homicide.

Liam was a performer, an Irish folk singer. He was displaying his talents for the prison guards on the day Joseph Sullivan escaped from Attica prison. It was that very distraction that allowed Sullivan to be buried under sacks of flour in a vehicle leaving the prison. The guards were so engrossed in Liam's performance that they waved the truck on (out of the prison) without searching it first. (75)

The Rochester Mob Wars - A,B&C Teams

The A-Team:

Sam (Red) Russotti
Salvatore (Sammy G) Gingello
Rene (The Painter) Piccarreto
Dick (Molly) Marino
Salvatore (Sam Camps) Campanella (defected to B Team)
Eugene (Gene the Firecracker) DeFrancesco
Dominic (Trigger Dom) Taddeo
Anthony Colombo
Joe (Joey T) Trieste
John (Johnny Flap) Trivigno
Tommy Marotta
Loren Piccarreto
Angelo Amico
Joseph (Joe the Hop) Rossi
Anthony (Tony Dags) D'Agostino
Nick (Bugsy the Fence) Fosco
Lou (Louie Tree Tops) Imburgia
Joseph (Joe the Genie) Geniola
Joseph (Joe Desserts) La Dolce
Anthony Oliveri
Bobby Palmiere
Joe (Joey Tubes) Tiraborelli
Don (Monroe Street Donnie) Paone
Orlando (Orlie P) Paone
Lou (Yamaha Louie) Santonato
Robert (Bobby Fernwood) Silveri

The B-Team

Tommy Didio
Dominic (Sonny) Celestino
Charles (Charlie the Ox) Indovino
Frank (Frankie the Farmer) Frassetto
Angelo Vaccaro
Jimmy Cannarozza
Rosario Chirico
Tony Chirico
Rodney Starkweather
Billy Barton
Vinnie Tobacco
Vincenzo (Vinnie the Captain) Cottone
Jimmy (Crazy Carlos) Bates

The C-Team

Tommy Torpey
Tommy Taylor
Louie DiGuilio
Bobby Comfort
Paul Comfort
Ray Sampson
Nicky Mastrodonato
Gerry, Tommy and Mike Pelusio
Liam Magee

Other books by the authors:

"The Rochester Mob Wars"
By Blair T. Kenny
© 2017

"The Rochester Mob Wars" is the true story about the rise and fall of the Rochester Mafia. The Rochester Mafia Crime Family boasted over 40 "made" members in its heyday, before internal strife and power struggles led to its demise by self destruction via murder, shootings, and bombings.

"The Rochester Mob Wars" book is the result of two years of research into organized crime in Rochester, New York. The book is a compilation of newspaper clippings, court documents and Senate Hearings placed in chronological order detailing the highlights of the Mob's activity over a 40 year period. The 208 page book covers the time period of the 1950's to 1997, when Teamsters Local #398 was put into "Trusteeship" for lifetime affiliation with the Mafia.

Other books by the authors:

"The Black Hand Society of Rochester"

By Blair T. Kenny

© 2019

"**The Black Hand Society of Rochester**" is the prequel to "The Rochester Mob Wars." Beginning with Italian Immigration, the 342 page book uncovers the origins of the Rochester Mafia, which had its roots in the Italian Camorra and their American branch called "The Black Hand." In similar fashion to the Mob Wars book, "The Black Hand Society of Rochester" documents organized criminal activities of Rochester mobsters from 1900-1948. The book comes complete with an index of more than 600 names and eight pages of mobster profiles.

therochestermobwars.com

Other books by the authors:

"The Hammer Conspiracies"

By Frank A. Aloi

© 1982

"The Hammer Conspiracies" details investigations of Mafia activity in Rochester, New York, the subsequent trials, and the debacle that followed. It is a story of perjured detectives, gang wars, organized crime, overthrown convictions, imprisoned law enforcement officers and prosecutors, faulty police work, and corrupt officials.

Vincent 'Jimmy the Hammer' Massaro was hit by the mob. His death generated conspiracy prosecutions against what was alleged to be the top echelon of the organization in Rochester, New York. The testimony of informers, including two of the alleged triggermen, and detectives who surveilled mob meetings where Massaro's fate was plotted produced convictions. But there had been no surveillances. Detectives admitted perjuring themselves. Alleged mobsters were released from prison. A bloody gang war erupted, and Federal Indictments were returned against Detectives and Prosecutors. A saga of fabricated evidence and corruption unprecedented in the war against organized crime.

*****

A special thank you goes to my editor, and friend, Wendy Post who spent her entire 2020 winter vacation, in Florida, editing this book. She is the full time Editor for The Owego Pennysaver newspaper in Owego, N.Y. Wendy contributed both her time and her editing skills, on short notice, in order to help make this book a success. Her work speaks for itself and is greatly appreciated.

Blair T. Kenny